𝔐errill's 𝔈nglish 𝔗exts

POEMS

BY

ROBERT BROWNING

EDITED WITH AN INTRODUCTION AND NOTES
BY CORNELIA BEARE, INSTRUCTOR IN ENGLISH,
WADLEIGH HIGH SCHOOL, NEW YORK CITY

NEW YORK
CHARLES E. MERRILL CO.

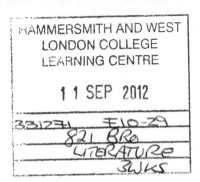
PUBLISHERS' NOTE

𝕸errill's 𝕰nglish 𝕿exts

THIS series of books will include in complete editions those masterpieces of English Literature that are best adapted for the use of schools and colleges. The editors of the several volumes will be chosen for their special qualifications in connection with the texts to be issued under their individual supervision, but familiarity with the practical needs of the classroom, no less than sound scholarship, will characterize the editing of every book in the series.

In connection with each text, a critical and historical introduction, including a sketch of the life of the author and his relation to the thought of his time, critical opinions of the work in question chosen from the great body of English criticism, and, where possible, a portrait of the author, will be given. Ample explanatory notes of such passages in the text as call for special attention will be supplied, but irrelevant annotation and explanations of the obvious will be rigidly excluded.

CHARLES E. MERRILL CO.

---

[12]

This portrait was executed at Rome, in 1859,
as a companion to that of E. B. B. now in the
National Portrait Gallery, by Field Talfourd,—whose
property it remained. I rejoice that it now belongs
to my friend Gosse. Robert Browning,
Apr. 10ᵗʰ 85.

CONTENTS

3

The poems mentioned for College Entrance Requirements in English for 1923–1928 are:

Cavalier Tunes, The Lost Leader, How They Brought the Good News from Ghent to Aix, Home Thoughts from Abroad, Home Thoughts from the Sea, Incident of the French Camp, Hervé Riel, Pheidippides, My Last Duchess, Up at a Villa—Down in the City, The Italian in England, The Patriot, "De Gustibus—," The Pied Piper, and Instans Tyrannus.

INTRODUCTION

ROBERT BROWNING

ROBERT BROWNING was born at Camberwell, a suburb of London, May 7, 1812. From his earliest years he was fond of writing verses, and, when twelve years of age, had produced poems enough to form a volume. His first published poem, *Pauline*, appeared in 1833, but his real introduction to the public was through *Paracelsus*, a drama, published in 1835. In 1837 the tragedy of *Strafford* was unsuccessfully presented at Drury Lane Theater. In 1840 the epic *Sordello* was published — one of his most characteristic and most difficult works. In 1841–46 appeared the series of *Bells and Pomegranates*, in eight shilling parts, containing much of his finest poetry, including the tragedy *A Blot on the 'Scutcheon* and the graceful dramatic poem *Pippa Passes*. In 1846 he was married to the distinguished poetess, Elizabeth Barrett, and soon after established his home in Italy. *Christmas Eve and Easter Day* appeared in 1850, followed by two volumes of short poems, *Men and Women*, 1855, and *Dramatis Personæ*, 1864. His greatest work, *The Ring and the Book*, appeared in 1868–69, closely followed by many other important poems, chief of which are *Fifine at the Fair*, 1872; *Red Cotton Night-cap Country*, 1873; *Aristophanes' Apology* and *The Inn Album*, 1875. Most important of his latest works are *Dramatic Idyls*, 1879–80; *Jocoseria*, 1883; *Ferishtah's Fancies*, 1885; *Parleyings with Certain People of Importance in their Day*, 1887; and *Asolando*, 1889. He died at Venice, May 12, 1889.

The first and perhaps the final impression we receive from the works of Robert Browning is that of a great nature, an immense personality. The poet in him is made up of many men. He is dramatist, humorist, lyrist, painter, musician, philosopher, and scholar, each in full measure, and he includes and dominates them all. In richness of nature, in scope and penetration of mind and vision, in all the potentialities of poetry, he is probably second among English poets to Shakespeare alone. In art, in the power of the patience of working his native ore, he is surpassed by many; but few have ever held so rich a mine in fee. He has written more than any other English poet with the exception of Shakespeare, and he comes very near the gigantic total of Shakespeare. His works are not a mere collection of poems, they are a literature. And his literature is the richest of modern times. If "the best poetry is that which reproduces the most of life," his place is among the great poets of the world. In the vast extent of his work he has dealt with or touched on nearly every phase and feature of humanity, and his scope is bounded only by the soul's limits and the last reaches of life. There are for him but two realities and but two subjects, Life and Thought. On these are expended all his imagination and all his intellect, more consistently and in a higher degree than can be said of any English poet since the age of Elizabeth. Life and thought, the dramatic and the metaphysical, are not considered apart, but woven into one seamless tissue; and in regard to both he has one point of view and one manner of treatment. It is this that causes the unity which subsists throughout his works, and it is this, too, which distinguishes him among poets, and makes that originality by virtue of which he has been described as the most striking figure in our poetic literature.

Most poets endeavor to sink the individual in the universal; it is the special distinction of Mr. Browning that when he is most universal he is most individual. As a thinker he conceives of humanity not as an aggregate, but as a collection of units. Most thinkers write and speak of man; Mr. Browning of men. With man as a species, with man as a society, he does not concern himself, but with individual man and man. Every man is for him an epitome of the universe, a center of creation. Life exists for each as completely and separately as if he were the only inhabitant of our planet.

Here it is that Mr. Browning parts company most decisively with all other poets who concern themselves exclusively with life — dramatic poets, as we call them; so that it seems almost necessary to invent some new term to define precisely his special attitude. And hence it is that in his drama thought plays comparatively so large, and action comparatively so small, a part; hence, that action is valued only in so far as it reveals thought or motive, not for its own sake, as the crown and flower of these. For his endeavor is not to set men in action for the pleasure of seeing them move; but to see and show, in their action and inaction alike, the real impulses of their being: to see how each soul conceives of itself.

The dramatic poet, in the ordinary sense, in the sense in which we apply it to Shakespeare and the Elizabethans, aims at showing, by means of action, the development of character as it manifests itself to the world in deeds. His study is character, but it is character in action, considered only in connection with a particular grouping of events, and only so far as it produces or operates upon these. The processes are concealed from us, we see the result. We are told nothing, we care to know nothing, of what is going on in the thought; of the infinitely subtle meshes of motive or emotion which will perhaps find no direct outcome in speech, no direct manifestation in action, but by which the soul's life in reality subsists.

But is there no other sense in which a poet may be dramatic, besides this sense of the acting drama? no new form possible, which

> "peradventure may outgrow
> The simulation of the painted scene,
> Boards, actors, prompters, gaslight, and costume,
> And take for a noble stage the soul itself,
> Its shifting fancies and celestial lights,
> With all its grand orchestral silences,
> To keep the pauses of the rhythmic sounds?" [1]

This new form of drama is the drama as we see it in Mr. Browning — a drama of the interior, a tragedy or comedy of the soul. Instead of a grouping of characters which shall act on one another to produce a certain result in action, we have a grouping of events useful or important only as they influence the character or the mind. In this way, by making the soul the center of action, he is enabled (thinking himself into it, as all dramatists must do) to bring out its characteristics, to reveal its very nature.

This, then, is Mr. Browning's consistent mental attitude, and his special method. But he has also a special instrument — the monologue. The drama of action demands a concurrence of several distinct personalities, influencing one another rapidly by word or deed, so as to bring about the catastrophe; hence the propriety of the dialogue. But the introspective drama, in which the design is to represent and reveal the individual, requires a concentration of interests, a focusing of light on one point, to the exclusion or subordination of surroundings; hence the propriety of the monologue, in which a single speaker or thinker can consciously or unconsciously exhibit his own soul. Nearly all the lyrics,

[1] *Aurora Leigh*, Book Fifth.

romances, idyls — nearly all the miscellaneous poems, long and short — are monologues.

The characteristic of which I have been speaking — the persistent care for the individual and personal, as distinguished from the universal and general — while it is the secret of his finest achievements, and rightly his special charm, is of all things the most alien to the ordinary conceptions of poetry, and the usual preferences for it. Compare, altogether apart from the worth and workmanship, one of Lord Tennyson's with one of Mr. Browning's best lyrics. The perfection of the former consists in the exquisite way in which it expresses feelings common to all. The perfection of the latter consists in the intensity of its expression of a single moment of passion or emotion; one peculiar to a single personality, and to that personality only at such a single moment. To appreciate it we must enter keenly and instantaneously into the imaginary character at its imagined crisis; and, even when this is easiest to do, it is evident that there must be more difficulty in doing it — for it requires a certain exertion — than in merely letting the mind lie at rest, accepting and absorbing.

Allied to Mr. Browning's originality in temper, topic, manner of treatment, and special form, is his originality in style. His style is vital; his verse moves to the throbbing of an inner organism, not to the pulsations of a machine. He prefers, as indeed all true poets do, but more exclusively than any other poet, sense to sound, thought to expression. In his desire of condensation he employs as few words as are consistent with the right expression of his thought; he rejects superlative adjectives and all stop-gap words. He refuses to use words for words' sake; he declines to interrupt conversation with a display of fireworks; and, as a result, it will be found that his finest effects of versification correspond with his highest achievements in imagination and passion. As a dramatic poet he is obliged to modulate and moderate, sometimes even to vulgarize, his style and diction for the proper expression of some particular character, in whose mouth exquisite turns of phrase and delicate felicities of rhythm would be inappropriate. He will not *let himself go* in the way of easy floridity, as writers may whose themes are more "ideal." And where many writers would attempt merely to simplify and sweeten verse, he endeavors to give it fuller expressiveness, to give it strength and newness. It follows that Mr. Browning's verse is not so uniformly melodious as that of many other poets. But he is far, indeed, from paying no attention, or little, to meter and versification. In one very important matter, that of rhyme, he is perhaps the greatest master in our language; in single and double, in simple and grotesque alike, he succeeds in fitting rhyme to rhyme with a perfection which I have never found in any other poet of any age. His lyrical poems contain more structural varieties of form than those of any preceding English poet, not excepting Shelley. His blank verse at its best is of higher quality — taking it for what it is, dramatic blank verse — than that of any other modern poet. And both in rhymed and in blank verse he has written passages which for almost every quality of verse are hardly to be surpassed in the language.

That there is some excuse for the charge of "obscurity" so often brought against Mr. Browning, no one would or could deny. But it is only the excuse of a misconception. Mr. Browning is a thinker of extraordinary depth and subtlety; his themes are seldom superficial, often very remote, and his thought is, moreover, as swift as it is subtle. To a dull reader there is little difference between cloudy and fiery thought; the one is as much too bright for him as the other is too dense. Of all thinkers in poetry, Mr. Browning is the most swift and fiery. Moreover, while a writer who deals with easy themes has no excuse if he is not pellucid to a glance, one who employs his intellect and imagination on high and hard questions has a right to demand a corresponding closeness of attention.

When Mr. Browning was a mere boy, it is recorded that he debated within himself whether he should not become a painter or a musician as well as a poet. Finally, though not, I believe, for a good many years, he decided in the negative. But the latent qualities of painter and musician have developed themselves in his poetry, and much of his finest and very much of his most original verse is that which speaks the language of painter and musician as it had never before been spoken. No English poet before him has ever excelled his utterances on music, none has so much as rivaled his utterances on art. In his poems on the sister arts of painting and sculpture — not in themselves more perfect in sympathy, though far greater in number, than those on music — he is simply the first to write of these arts as an artist might, if he could express his soul in words or rhythm.

It is only natural that a poet with the instincts of a painter should be capable of superb landscape painting in verse; and we find in Mr. Browning this power. It is further evident that such a poet — a man who has chosen poetry instead of painting — must consider the latter art subordinate to the former, and it is only natural that we should find Mr. Browning subordinating the pictorial to the poetic capacity, and this more carefully than most other poets. His best landscapes are as brief as they are brilliant. They are as saber-strokes, swift, sudden, flashing the light from their sweep, and striking straight to the heart. And they are never pushed into prominence for an effect of ideal beauty, nor strewn about in the way of thoughtful or passionate utterance, like roses in a runner's path. They are subordinated always to the human interest; blended, *fused* with it, so that a landscape in a poem of Mr. Browning's is literally a part of the emotion.

Of all poets Mr. Browning is the healthiest and manliest. His genius is robust with vigorous blood, and his tone has the cheeriness of intellectual health. The most subtle of minds, his is the least sickly. The wind that blows in his pages is no hot or languorous breeze, laden with scents and sweets, but a fresh salt wind blowing in from the sea. The keynote of his philosophy is:

> "God's in his heaven,
> All's right with the world!"

He has such a hopefulness of belief in human nature that he shrinks from no *man*, however clothed and cloaked in evil, however miry with stumblings and fallings. This vivid hope and trust in man is bound up with a strong and strenuous faith in God. Mr. Browning's Christianity is wider than our creeds, and is all the more vitally Christian in that it never sinks into pietism. He is never didactic, but his faith is the root of his art, and transforms and transfigures it. Yet as a dramatic poet he is so impartial, and can express all creeds with so easy an interpretative accent, that it is possible to prove him (as Shakespeare has been proved) a believer in everything and a disbeliever in anything.

Condensed from "Introduction to Study of Browning" by Arthur Symons.

CRITICAL OPINIONS

I can have little doubt that my writing has been in the main too hard for many I should have been pleased to communicate with; but I never designedly tried to puzzle people, as some of my critics have supposed. On the other hand, I never pretended to offer such literature as should be a substitute for a cigar or a game at dominoes to an idle man. So, perhaps, on the whole I get my deserts and something over — not a crowd, but a few I value more. — *Robert Browning to W. G. Kingsland.*

Browning, when, in poem or drama, he puts forth his peculiar power, when he writes with the motive which gives his work its singular value, is always dramatic. Whether he is so of purpose I shall not venture to say: but the seeming of his poetry is that it takes its shape from a necessity of his moral nature, not from deliberate intellectual preference. He never seems to be telling us what he thinks or feels; but he puts before us some man, — male or female, — whose individuality soon becomes as clear and as absolute as our own; and that man pours his heart and soul out before us in words which are a part of him, utterly careless of what we think of the life whose hidden motives are thus laid bare to censure. The poet does not appear; indeed so wholly is he merged in the creature of his own will that, as we hear that creature speak, his creator is, for the time, quite forgotten. This is the perfection of dramatic power. It has been shown with this high absoluteness in English poetry by but two men, one of whom is Browning. — *Richard Grant White.*

Man here on earth, according to the central and controlling thought of Mr. Browning, man here in a state of preparation for other lives, and surrounded by wondrous spiritual influences, is too great for the sphere that contains him, while, at the same time, he can exist only by submitting for the present to the conditions it imposes; never without fatal loss becoming content with submission, or regarding his present state as perfect or final. Our nature here is unfinished, imperfect, but its glory, its peculiarity, that which makes us men — not God, and not brutes — lies precisely in this character of imperfection, giving scope as it does for indefinite growth and progress.

"Progress, man's distinctive mark alone, not God's, and not the beasts'; God is, they are, man partly is, and wholly hopes to be." . . .

With Mr. Browning the moments are most glorious in which the obscure tendency of many years has been revealed by the lightning of sudden passion, or in which a resolution that changes the current of life has been taken in reliance upon that insight which vivid emotion bestows; and those periods of our history are charged most fully with moral purpose which take their direction from moments such as these. — *Edward Dowden.*

If there is any great quality more perceptible than another in Mr. Browning's intellect, it is his decisive and incisive faculty of thought, his sureness and intensity of perception, his rapid and trenchant resolution of aim. To charge him with obscurity is about as accurate as to call Lynceus purblind, or complain of the sluggish action of the telegraphic wire. He is something too much the reverse of obscure; he is too brilliant and subtle for the ready reader of a ready writer to follow with any certainty the track of intelligence which moves with such incessant rapidity. . . . The very essence of Mr. Browning's aim and method, as exhibited in the ripest fruits of his intelligence, is such as implies above all other things the possession of a quality the very reverse of obscurity — a faculty of spiritual illumination rapid and intense and subtle as lightning, which brings to bear upon its central object by way of direct and vivid illustration every symbol and detail on which its light is flashed in passing. — *A. C. Swinburne.*

CAVALIER TUNES

I

CAVALIER TUNES [1]

I

KENTISH Sir Byng stood for his King,
Bidding the crop-headed Parliament swing:
And, pressing a troop unable to stoop
And see the rogues flourish and honest folk droop,
Marched them along, fifty-score strong,
Great-hearted gentlemen, singing this song.

II

God for King Charles! Pym [2] and such carles [3]
To the Devil that prompts 'em their treasonous
    parles! [4]
Cavaliers, up! Lips from the cup,
Hands from the pasty, nor bite take nor sup,
Till you're —

    (Chorus) *Marching along, fifty-score strong,*
            Great-hearted gentlemen, singing this song.

III

Hampden to hell, and his obsequies' knell
Serve Hazelrig, Fiennes, and young Harry as well!
England, good cheer!   Rupert is near!
Kentish and loyalist, keep we not here,

   (Chorus) *Marching along, fifty-score strong,*
          Great-hearted gentlemen, singing this song.

IV

Then, God for King Charles!   Pym and his snarls
To the Devil that pricks on such pestilent carles!
Hold by the right, you double your might;
So, onward to Nottingham, fresh for the fight,

   (Chorus) *March we along, fifty-score strong,*
          Great-hearted gentlemen, singing this song!

II

GIVE A ROUSE [1]

I

KING CHARLES, and who'll do him right now?
King Charles, and who's ripe for fight now?
Give a rouse: here's, in hell's despite now,
King Charles!

II

Who gave me the goods that went since?
Who raised me the house that sank once?
Who helped me to gold I spent since?
Who found me in wine you drank once?
  (Chorus) *King Charles, and who'll do him right now?*
       King Charles, and who's ripe for fight now?
       Give a rouse: here's, in hell's despite now,
       King Charles!

III

To whom used my boy George quaff else,
By the old fool's side that begot him?
For whom did he cheer and laugh else,
While Noll's [1] damned troopers shot him?
  (Chorus) *King Charles, and who'll do him right now?*
       King Charles, and who's ripe for fight now?
       Give a rouse: here's, in hell's despite now,
       King Charles!

III

BOOT AND SADDLE

I

Boot, saddle, to horse, and away!
Rescue my castle before the hot day
Brightens to blue from its silvery gray,
    (Chorus) *"Boot, saddle, to horse, and away!"*

II

Ride past the suburbs, asleep as you'd say;
Many's the friend there, will listen and pray
"God's luck to gallants that strike up the lay —
  (Chorus) "*Boot, saddle, to horse, and away!*"

III

Forty miles off, like a roebuck at bay,
Flouts [1] Castle Brancepeth the Roundheads' array:
Who laughs, "Good fellows ere this, by my fay,[2]
  (Chorus) "*Boot, saddle, to horse, and away!*"

IV

Who?   My wife Gertrude; that, honest and gay,
Laughs when you talk of surrendering, "Nay!
I've better counselors; what counsel they?
  (Chorus) "*Boot, saddle, to horse, and away!*"

THE LOST LEADER

The Lost Leader was originally written in reference to
Wordsworth's abandonment of the Liberal cause, with per-
haps a thought of Southey, but it is applicable to any popular
apostasy.   This is one of those songs that do the work of
swords.   It shows how easily Browning, had he so chosen,
could have stirred the national feeling with his lyrics.

Just for a handful of silver he left us,
  Just for a riband to stick in his coat —

Found the one gift of which fortune bereft us,
    Lost all the others, she lets us devote;
They, with the gold to give, doled him out silver,
    So much was theirs who so little allowed:
How all our copper had gone for his service!
    Rags — were they purple, his heart had been
        proud!
We that had loved him so, followed him, honored
        him,
    Lived in his mild and magnificent eye,
Learned his great language, caught his clear ac-
        cents,
    Made him our pattern to live and to die!
Shakespeare was of us, Milton was for us,
    Burns, Shelley, were with us, — they watch from
        their graves!
He alone breaks from the van and the freemen,
    He alone sinks to the rear and the slaves!

We shall march prospering, — not through his
    presence;
    Songs may inspirit us, — not from his lyre;
Deeds will be done, — while he boasts his quies-
    cence,
    Still bidding crouch whom the rest bade aspire:
Blot out his name, then, record one lost soul more,

One task more declined, one more footpath un-
    trod,
One more devils'-triumph and sorrow for angels,
    One wrong more to man, one more insult to God!
Life's night begins: let him never come back to us!
    There would be doubt, hesitation and pain,
Forced praise on our part — the glimmer of twi-
    light,
    Never glad confident morning again!
Best fight on well, for we taught him — strike
    gallantly,
    Menace our heart ere we master his own;
Then let him receive the new knowledge and wait us,
    Pardoned in heaven, the first by the throne!

"HOW THEY BROUGHT THE GOOD NEWS
FROM GHENT TO AIX"

The "good news" of this stirring ballad is intended for
that of the Pacification of Ghent, a treaty of union entered
into by Holland, Zealand, and the southern Netherlands
against the tyrannical Philip II., in 1576. The incident of
the poem is not historical. "I wrote it," says Browning,
"under the bulwark of a vessel off the African coast, after
I had been at sea long enough to appreciate even the fancy
of a gallop on the back of a certain good horse 'York' then
in my stable at home."

I SPRANG to the stirrup, and Joris, and he;
I galloped, Dirck galloped, we galloped all three;

"Good speed!" cried the watch, as the gate-bolts
  undrew;
"Speed!" echoed the wall to us galloping through;
Behind shut the postern, the lights sank to rest,
And into the midnight we galloped abreast.

Not a word to each other; we kept the great pace
Neck by neck, stride by stride, never changing our
  place;
I turned in my saddle and made its girths tight,
Then shortened each stirrup, and set the pique [1]
  right,
Rebuckled the cheek-strap, chained slacker the bit,
Nor galloped less steadily Roland a whit.

'Twas moonset at starting; but while we drew near
Lokeren,[2] the cocks crew and twilight dawned clear;
At Boom, a great yellow star came out to see;
At Düffeld, 'twas morning as plain as could be;
And from Mecheln [3] church-steeple we heard the
  half chime,
So Joris broke silence with, "Yet there is time!"

At Aershot, up leaped of a sudden the sun,
And against him the cattle stood black every one,
To stare through the mist at us galloping past,

And I saw my stout galloper Roland at last,
With resolute shoulders, each butting away
The haze, as some bluff river headland its spray:

And his low head and crest, just one sharp ear bent
    back
For my voice, and the other pricked out on his
    track;
And one eye's black intelligence, — ever that
    glance
O'er its white edge at me, his own master, askance!
And the thick heavy spume-flakes which aye and
    anon
His fierce lips shook upwards in galloping on.

By Hasselt, Dirck groaned; and cried Joris, "Stay
    spur"
Your Roos galloped bravely, the fault's not in her,
We'll remember at Aix" — for one heard the quick
    wheeze
Of her chest, saw the stretched neck and staggering
    knees,
And sunk tail, and horrible heave of the flank,
As down on her haunches she shuddered and sank.

So we were left galloping, Joris and I,

Past Looz and past Tongres, no cloud in the sky;
The broad sun above laughed a pitiless laugh,
'Neath our feet broke the brittle bright stubble like
    chaff;
Till over by Dalhem [1] a dome-spire sprang white,
And "Gallop," gasped Joris, "for Aix is in sight!"

"How they'll greet us!" — and all in a moment his
    roan
Rolled neck and croup over, lay dead as a stone;
And there was my Roland to bear the whole weight
Of the news which alone could save Aix from her
    fate,[2]
With his nostrils like pits full of blood to the brim,
And circles of red for his eye-sockets' rim.

Then I cast loose my buff-coat, each holster let fall,
Shook off both my jack-boots, let go belt and all,
Stood up in the stirrup, leaned, patted his ear,
Called my Roland his pet-name, my horse without
    peer;
Clapped my hands, laughed and sang, any noise,
    bad or good,
Till at length into Aix Roland galloped and stood.

And all I remember is, friends flocking round

As I sat with his head 'twixt my knees on the
    ground;
And no voice but was praising this Roland of mine,
As I poured down his throat our last measure of
    wine,
Which (the burgesses voted by common consent)
Was no more than his due who brought good news
    from Ghent.

EVELYN HOPE

BEAUTIFUL Evelyn Hope is dead!
    Sit and watch by her side an hour.
That is her book-shelf, this her bed;
    She plucked that piece of geranium-flower,
Beginning to die too, in the glass;
    Little has yet been changed, I think;
The shutters are shut, no light may pass
    Save two long rays through the hinge's chink.

Sixteen years old when she died!
    Perhaps she had scarcely heard my name;
It was not her time to love; beside,
    Her life had many a hope and aim,
Duties enough, and little cares,
    And now was quiet, now astir,

Till God's hand beckoned unawares, —
  And the sweet white brow is all of her.

Is it too late, then, Evelyn Hope?
  What, your soul was pure and true,
The good stars met in your horoscope,
  Made you of spirit, fire and dew —
And, just because I was thrice as old
  And our paths in the world diverged so wide,
Each was naught to each, must I be told?
  We were fellow mortals, naught beside?

No, indeed! for God above
  Is great to grant, as mighty to make,
And creates the love to reward the love:
  I claim you still, for my own love's sake!
Delayed it may be for more lives yet,
  Through worlds I shall traverse, not a few:
Much is to learn, much to forget,
  Ere the time be come for taking you.

But the time will come, — at last it will,
  When, Evelyn Hope, what meant (I shall say)
In the lower earth, in the years long still,
  That body and soul so pure and gay?
Why your hair was amber, I shall divine,

And your mouth of your own geranium's red —
And what you would do with me, in fine,
  In the new life come in the old one's stead.

I have lived (I shall say) so much since then,
  Given up myself so many times,
Gained me the gains of various men,
  Ransacked the ages, spoiled the climes;
Yet one thing, one, in my soul's full scope,
  Either I missed or itself missed me:
And I want and find you, Evelyn Hope!
  What is the issue? let us see!

I loved you, Evelyn, all the while!
  My heart seemed full as it could hold;
There was place and to spare for the frank young
    smile,
  And the red young mouth, and the hair's young
    gold.
So, hush, — I will give you this leaf to keep:
  See, I shut it inside the sweet cold hand!
There, that is our secret: go to sleep!
  You will wake, and remember, and understand.

HOME THOUGHTS, FROM ABROAD

OH, to be in England now that April's there,
And whoever wakes in England sees, some morning,
    unaware,
That the lowest boughs and the brushwood sheaf
Round the elm-tree bole are in tiny leaf,
While the chaffinch sings on the orchard bough
In England — now!
And after April, when May follows,
And the white-throat builds, and all the swallows!
Hark, where my blossomed pear-tree in the hedge
Leans to the field and scatters on the clover
Blossoms and dewdrops — at the bent spray's
    edge —
That's the wise thrush: he sings each song twice
    over
Lest you should think he never could recapture
The first fine careless rapture!
And though the fields look rough with hoary dew,
All will be gay when noontide wakes anew
The buttercups, the little children's dower
— Far brighter than this gaudy melon-flower!

HOME–THOUGHTS, FROM THE SEA [1]

NOBLY, nobly Cape Saint Vincent to the Northwest
    died away;
Sunset ran, one glorious blood-red, reeking into
    Cadiz Bay;
Bluish 'mid the burning water, full in face Trafal-
    gar lay;
In the dimmest Northeast distance dawned Gib-
    raltar grand and gray;

"Here and here did England help me: how can I
    help England?" — say,
Whoso turns as I, this evening, turn to God to
    praise and pray
While Jove's planet rises yonder, silent over Africa.

INCIDENT OF THE FRENCH CAMP

YOU know, we French stormed Ratisbon: [2]
    A mile or so away
On a little mound, Napoleon
    Stood on our storming-day;
With neck out-thrust, you fancy how,
    Legs wide, arms locked behind,
As if to balance the prone brow
    Oppressive with its mind.

Just as perhaps he mused "My plans
   That soar, to earth may fall,
Let once my army-leader Lannes [1]
   Waver at yonder wall," —
Out 'twixt the battery-smokes there flew
   A rider, bound on bound
Full-galloping; nor bridle drew
   Until he reached the mound.

Then off there flung in smiling joy,
   And held himself erect
By just his horse's mane, a boy:
   You hardly could suspect —
(So tight he kept his lips compressed,
   Scarce any blood came through)
You looked twice ere you saw his breast
   Was all but shot in two.

"Well," cried he, "Emperor, by God's grace
   We've got you Ratisbon!
The Marshal's in the market-place,
   And you'll be there anon
To see your flag-bird flap his vans [2].
   Where I, to heart's desire,
Perched him!" The chief's eye flashed; his plans
   Soared up again like fire.

The chief's eye flashed; but presently
　　Softened itself, as sheathes
A film the mother-eagle's eye
　　When her bruised eaglet breathes;
"You're wounded!"　"Nay," the soldier's pride
　　Touched to the quick, he said:
"I'm killed, Sire!"　And his chief beside,
　　Smiling the boy fell dead.

THE BOY AND THE ANGEL

Morning, evening, noon and night,
"Praise God!" sang Theocrite.

Then to his poor trade he turned,
Whereby the daily meal was earned.

Hard he labored, long and well;
O'er his work the boy's curls fell:

But ever, at each period,
He stopped and sang, "Praise God!"

Then back again his curls he threw,
And cheerful turned to work anew.

Said Blaise, the listening monk, "Well done;
I doubt not thou art heard, my son:

"As well as if thy voice to-day
Were praising God the Pope's great way.

"This Easter Day, the Pope at Rome
Praises God from Peter's dome."

Said Theocrite, "Would God that I
Might praise him, that great way, and die!"

Night passed, day shone,
And Theocrite was gone.

With God a day endures alway,
A thousand years are but a day.

God said in heaven, "Nor day nor night
Now brings the voice of my delight."

Then Gabriel, like a rainbow's birth,
Spread his wings and sank to earth;

Entered, in flesh, the empty cell,
Lived there, and played the craftsman well;

And morning, evening, noon and night,
Praised God in place of Theocrite.

And from a boy to youth he grew:
The man put off the stripling's hue:

The man matured and fell away
Into the season of decay:

And ever o'er the trade he bent,
And ever lived on earth content.

(He did God's will; to him, all one
If on the earth or in the sun.)

God said, "A praise is in mine ear;
There is no doubt in it, no fear:

"So sing old worlds, and so
New worlds that from my footstool go.

"Clearer loves sound other ways:
I miss my little human praise."

Then forth sprang Gabriel's wings, off fell
The flesh disguise, remained the cell.

'Twas Easter Day: he flew to Rome,
And paused above Saint Peter's dome.

In the tiring-room [1] close by
The great outer gallery,

With his holy vestments dight,
Stood the new Pope, Theocrite:

And all his past career
Came back upon him clear,

Since when, a boy, he plied his trade,
Till on his life the sickness weighed:

And in his cell, when death drew near,
An angel in a dream brought cheer:

And rising from the sickness drear,
He grew a priest, and now stood here.

To the East with praise he turned,
And on his sight the angel burned.

"I bore thee from thy craftsman's cell,
And set thee here; I did not well.

"Vainly I left my angel-sphere,
Vain was thy dream of many a year.

"Thy voice's praise seemed weak; it dropped —
Creation's chorus stopped!

"Go back and praise again
The early way, while I remain.

"With that weak voice of our disdain,
Take up creation's pausing strain.

" Back to the cell and poor employ:
Resume the craftsman and the boy!"

Theocrite grew old at home;
A new Pope dwelt in Peter's dome.

One vanished as the other died:
They sought God side by side.

ONE WORD MORE

I

THERE they are, my fifty men and women
Naming me the fifty poems finished!
Take them, Love, the book and me together:
Where the heart lies, let the brain lie also.

II

Rafael made a century of sonnets,
Made and wrote them in a certain volume
Dinted with the silver-pointed pencil
Else he only used to draw Madonnas:
These, the world might view — but one, the volume.
Who that one, you ask?   Your heart instructs you.
Did she live and love it all her lifetime?
Did she drop, his lady of the sonnets,
Die, and let it drop beside her pillow

Where it lay in place of Rafael's glory,
Rafael's cheek so duteous and so loving —
Cheek, the world was wont to hail a painter's,
Rafael's cheek, her love had turned a poet's?

III

You and I would rather read that volume,
(Taken to his beating bosom by it)
Lean and list the bosom-beats of Rafael,
Would we not? than wonder at Madonnas —
Her, San Sisto names, and Her, Foligno,
Her, that visits Florence in a vision,
Her, that's left with lilies in the Louvre [1] —
Seen by us and all the world in circle.[2]

IV

You and I will never read that volume.
Guido Reni, like his own eye's apple
Guarded long the treasure-book and loved it.
Guido Reni [3] dying, all Bologna
Cried, and the world too, "Ours, the treasure!"
Suddenly, as rare things will, it vanished.

V

Dante once prepared to paint an angel:
Whom to please? You whisper "Beatrice." [4]

While he mused and traced and retraced it,
(Peradventure with a pen corroded
Still by drops of that hot ink he dipped for,
When, his left hand i' the hair o' the wicked,
Back he held the brow and pricked its stigma,
Bit into the live man's flesh for parchment,
Loosed him, laughed to see the writing rankle,
Let the wretch go festering through Florence) —
Dante, who loved well because he hated,
Hated wickedness that hinders loving,
Dante standing, studying his angel, —
In there broke the folk of his Inferno.
Says he — "Certain people of importance"
(Such he gave his daily dreadful line to)
"Entered and would seize, forsooth, the poet."
Says the poet — "Then I stopped my painting."

VI

You and I would rather see that angel,
Painted by the tenderness of Dante,
Would we not? — than read a fresh Inferno.

VII

You and I will never see that picture.
While he mused on love and Beatrice,
While he softened o'er his outlined angel,

In they broke, those "people of importance":
We and Bice [1] bear the loss forever.

VIII

What of Rafael's sonnets, Dante's picture?
This: no artist lives and loves, that longs not
Once, and only once, and for one only
(Ah, the prize!) to find his love a language
Fit and fair and simple and sufficient —
Using nature that's an art to others,
Not, this one time, art that's turned his nature.
Ay, of all the artists living, loving,
None but would forego his proper dowry, —
Does he paint? he fain would write a poem, —
Does he write? he fain would paint a picture,
Put to proof art alien to the artist's,
Once, and only once, and for one only,
So to be the man and leave the artist,
Gain the man's joy, miss the artist's sorrow.

IX

Wherefore? Heaven's gift takes earth's abatement!
He who smites the rock and spreads the water, [2]
Bidding drink and live a crowd beneath him,
Even he, the minute makes immortal,
Proves, perchance, but mortal in the minute,

Desecrates, belike, the deed in doing.
While he smites, how can he but remember,
So he smote before, in such a peril,
When they stood and mocked — "Shall smiting
    help us?"
When they drank and sneered — "A stroke is
    easy!"
When they wiped their mouths and went their
    journey,
Throwing him for thanks — "But drought was
    pleasant."
Thus old memories mar the actual triumph;
Thus the doing savors of disrelish;
Thus achievement lacks a gracious somewhat;
O'er-importuned brows becloud the mandate,
Carelessness or consciousness — the gesture.
For he bears an ancient wrong about him,
Sees and knows again those phalanxed faces,
Hears, yet one time more, the 'customed pre-
    lude —
"How shouldst thou, of all men, smite, and save
    us?"
Guesses what is like to prove the sequel —
"Egypt's flesh-pots — nay, the drought was bet-
    ter."

X

Oh, the crowd must have emphatic warrant!
Theirs, the Sinai-forehead's [1] cloven brilliance,
Right-arm's rod-sweep, tongue's imperial fiat.
Never dares the man put off the prophet.

XI

Did he love one face from out the thousands,
(Were she Jethro's daughter,[2] white and wifely,
Were she but the Æthiopian bondslave,)
He would envy yon dumb patient camel,
Keeping a reserve of scanty water
Meant to save his own life in the desert;
Ready in the desert to deliver
(Kneeling down to let his breast be opened)
Hoard and life together for his mistress.

XII

I shall never, in the years remaining,
Paint you pictures, no, nor carve you statues,
Make you music that should all-express me;
So it seems: I stand on my attainment.
This of verse alone, one life allows me;
Verse and nothing else have I to give you.
Other heights in other lives, God willing:
All the gifts from all the heights, your own, Love!

XIII

Yet a semblance of resource avails us —
Shade so finely touched, love's sense must seize it.
Take these lines, look lovingly and nearly,
Lines I write the first time and the last time.
He who works in fresco, steals a hair-brush,
Curbs the liberal hand, subservient proudly,
Cramps his spirit, crowds it all in little,
Makes a strange art of an art familiar,
Fills his lady's missal-marge with flowerets.
He who blows through bronze, may breathe through
        silver,
Fitly serenade a slumbrous princess.
He who writes, may write for once as I do.

XIV

Love, you saw me gather men and women,
Live or dead or fashioned by my fancy,
Enter each and all, and use their service,
Speak from every mouth, — the speech, a poem,
Hardly shall I tell my joys and sorrows,
Hopes and fears, belief and disbelieving:
I am mine and yours — the rest be all men's,
Karshish,[1] Cleon, Norbert, and the fifty.
Let me speak this once in my true person,

Not as Lippo, Roland, or Andrea,
Though the fruit of speech be just this sentence:
Pray you, look on these my men and women,
Take and keep my fifty poems finished;
Where my heart lies, let my brain lie also!
Poor the speech; be how I speak, for all things.

XV

Not but that you know me! Lo, the moon's self!
Here in London, yonder late in Florence,
Still we find her face, the thrice-transfigured.
Curving on a sky imbrued with color,
Drifted over Fiesole ¹ by twilight,
Came she, our new crescent of a hair's-breadth.
Full she flared it, lamping Samminiato,²
Rounder 'twixt the cypresses and rounder,
Perfect till the nightingales applauded.
Now, a piece of her old self, impoverished,
Hard to greet, she traverses the house-roofs,
Hurries with unhandsome thrift of silver,
Goes dispiritedly, glad to finish.

XVI

What, there's nothing in the moon noteworthy?
Nay: for if that moon could love a mortal,
Use, to charm him (so to fit a fancy),

All her magic ('tis the old sweet mythos [1]),
She would turn a new side to her mortal,
Side unseen of herdsman, huntsman, steersman —
Blank to Zoroaster [2] on his terrace,
Blind to Galileo [3] on his turret,
Dumb to Homer, dumb to Keats — him, even!
Think, the wonder of the moonstruck mortal —
When she turns round, comes again in heaven,
Opens out anew for worse or better!
Proves she like some portent of an iceberg
Swimming full upon the ship it founders,
Hungry with huge teeth of splintered crystals?
Proves she as the paved work of a sapphire
Seen by Moses when he climbed the mountain?
Moses, Aaron, Nadab and Abihu [4]
Climbed and saw the very God, the Highest,
Stand upon the paved work of a sapphire.
Like the bodied heaven in his clearness
Shone the stone, the sapphire of that paved work,
When they ate and drank and saw God also!

XVII

What were seen? None knows, none ever shall
        know.
Only this is sure — the sight were other,
Not the moon's same side, born late in Florence,

Dying now impoverished here in London.
God be thanked, the meanest of his creatures
Boasts two soul-sides, one to face the world with,
One to show a woman when he loves her!

XVIII

This I say of me, but think of you, Love!
This to you — yourself my moon of poets!
Ah, but that's the world's side, there's the wonder.
Thus they see you, praise you, think they know
    you!
There, in turn I stand with them and praise you —
Out of my own self, I dare to phrase it.
But the best is when I glide from out them,
Cross a step or two of dubious twilight,
Come out on the other side, the novel
Silent silver lights and darks undreamed of,
Where I hush and bless myself with silence.

XIX

Oh, their Rafael of the dear Madonnas,
Oh, their Dante of the dread Inferno,
Wrote one song — and in my brain I sing it,
Drew one angel — borne, see, on my bosom!

HERVÉ RIEL [1]

I

On the sea and at the Hogue, sixteen hundred
    ninety-two,
  Did the English fight the French,— woe to France!
And, the thirty-first of May, helter-skelter thro'
    the blue,
Like a crowd of frightened porpoises a shoal of
    sharks pursue,
  Came crowding ship on ship to St. Malo [2] on the
    Rance,
With the English fleet in view.

II

'Twas the squadron that escaped, with the victor
    in full chase;
  First and foremost of the drove, in his great ship,
    Damfreville; [3]
    Close on him fled, great and small,
    Twenty-two good ships in all;
And they signaled to the place
"Help the winners of a race!
  Get us guidance, give us harbor, take us quick —
    or, quicker still,
  Here's the English can and will!"

III

Then the pilots of the place put out brisk and leapt
    on board;
  " Why, what hope or chance have ships like these
    to pass?" laughed they:
" Rocks to starboard, rocks to port, all the passage
    scarred and scored.
Shall the *Formidable* here with her twelve and
    eighty [1] guns
  Think to make the river-mouth by the single
    narrow way,
Trust to enter where 'tis ticklish for a craft of twenty
    tons,
    And with flow at full beside?
    Now 'tis slackest ebb of tide.
  Reach the mooring?   Rather say,
While rock stands or water runs,
Not a ship will leave the bay!"

IV

Then was called a council straight.
Brief and bitter the debate:
" Here's the English at our heels; would you have
    them take in tow
All that's left us of the fleet, linked together stern
    and bow,

For a prize to Plymouth [1] Sound?
Better run the ships aground!"
(Ended Damfreville his speech.)
Not a minute more to wait!
"Let the Captains all and each
Shove ashore, then blow up, burn the vessels
on the beach!
France must undergo her fate.

v

"Give the word!" But no such word
Was ever spoke or heard;
For up stood, for out stepped, for in struck amid
all these
— A Captain? A Lieutenant? A mate — first, sec-
ond, third?
No such man of mark, and meet
With his betters to compete!
But a simple Breton sailor pressed by Tourville [2]
for the fleet,
A poor coasting-pilot he, Hervé Riel the Croisickese. [3]

vi

And, "What mockery or malice have we here?"
cries Hervé Riel:
"Are you mad, you Malouins? [4] Are you cow-
ards, fools, or rogues?

Talk to me of rocks and shoals, me who took the
    soundings, tell
On my fingers every bank, every shallow, every
    swell
   'Twixt the offing here and Grève [1] where the river
     disembogues?
Are you bought by English gold? Is it love the
    lying's for?
   Morn and eve, night and day,
   Have I piloted your bay.
Entered free and anchored fast at the foot of Sol-
    idor. [2]
   Burn the fleet and ruin France? That were
     worse than fifty Hogues!
    Sirs, they know I speak the truth! Sirs, be-
     lieve me there's a way!
Only let me lead the line,
   Have the biggest ship to steer,
   Get this *Formidable* clear,
Make the others follow mine,
And I lead them, most and least, by a passage I
    know well,
   Right to Solidor past Grève,
    And there lay them safe and sound;
   And if one ship misbehave,
    — Keel so much as grate the ground,

Why, I've nothing but my life, — here's my head!"
    cries Hervé Riel.

VII

Not a minute more to wait.
"Steer us in, then, small and great!
  Take the helm, lead the line, save the squadron!"
    cried its chief.
Captains, give the sailor place!
  He is Admiral, in brief.
Still the north-wind, by God's grace!
See the noble fellow's face
As the big ship, with a bound,
Clears the entry like a hound,
Keeps the passage as its inch of way were the wide
    sea's profound!
  See, safe thro' shoal and rock,
  How they follow in a flock,
Not a ship that misbehaves, not a keel that grates
    the ground,
  Not a spar that comes to grief!
The peril, see, is past,
All are harbored to the last,
And just as Hervé Riel hollas "Anchor!" — sure
    as fate
Up the English come, too late!

VIII

So, the storm subsides to calm:
  They see the green trees wave
  On the heights o'erlooking Grève.
Hearts that bled are stanched with balm.
"Just our rapture to enhance,   .
  Let the English rake the bay,[1]
Gnash their teeth and glare askance
  As they cannonade away!
'Neath rampired[2] Solidor pleasant riding on the
    Rance!"
How hope succeeds despair on each Captain's coun-
    tenance!
Out burst all with one accord,
  "This is Paradise for Hell!
    Let France, let France's King
    Thank the man that did the thing!"
What a shout, and all one word,
  "Hervé Riel!"
As he stepped in front once more,
  Not a symptom of surprise
  In the frank blue Breton eyes,
Just the same man as before.

IX

Then said Damfreville, "My friend,
I must speak out at the end,
    Tho' I find the speaking hard.
Praise is deeper than the lips:
You have saved the King his ships,
    You must name your own reward.
'Faith our sun was near eclipse!
Demand whate'er you will,
France remains your debtor still.
Ask to heart's content and have! or my name's not
        Damfreville."

X

Then a beam of fun outbroke
On the bearded mouth that spoke,
As the honest heart laughed through
Those frank eyes of Breton blue:
"Since I needs must say my say,
    Since on board the duty's done,
    And from Malo Roads to Croisic Point, what is
        it but a run? —
Since 'tis ask and have, I may —
    Since the others go ashore —
Come!   A good whole holiday!

Leave to go and see my wife, whom I call the
     Belle Aurore!"
That he asked and that he got, — nothing more.

XI

Name and deed alike are lost:
Not a pillar nor a post
     In his Croisic keeps alive the feat as it befell;
Not a head in white and black
On a single fishing smack,
In memory of the man but for whom had gone to
     wrack [1]
     All that France saved from the fight whence Eng-
     land bore the bell. [2]
Go to Paris: rank on rank
     Search the heroes flung pell-mell
On the Louvre, [3] face and flank!
     You shall look long enough ere you come to Hervé
     Riel.
So, for better and for worse,
Hervé Riel, accept my verse!
In my verse, Hervé Riel, do thou once more
Save the squadron, honor France, love thy wife the
     Bell Aurore!

PHEIDIPPIDES [1]

χαίρετε νικῶμεν.

FIRST I salute this soil of the blessed, river and
   rock!
Gods of my birthplace, dæmons [2] and heroes, honor
   to all!
Then I name thee, claim thee for our patron, co-
   equal in praise
— Ay, with Zeus [3] the Defender, with Her of the
   ægis and spear!
Also ye of the bow and the buskin, [4] praised be your
   peer,
Now, henceforth and forever, — O latest to whom
   I upraise
Hand and heart and voice! For Athens, leave
   pasture and flock!
Present to help, potent to save, Pan [5] — patron I
   call!

Archons [6] of Athens, topped by the tettix, see, I
   return!
See, 'tis myself here standing alive, no specter that
   speaks!
Crowned with the myrtle, did you command me,
   Athens and you,

"Run, Pheidippides, run and race, reach Sparta
  for aid!
Persia has come, we are here, where is She?" Your
  command I obeyed,
Ran and raced: like stubble, some field which a fire
  runs through
Was the space between city and city; two days,
  two nights did I burn
Over the hills, under the dales, down pits and up
  peaks.
Into their midst I broke: breath served but for
  "Persia has come!
Persia bids Athens proffer slaves'-tribute, water
  and earth:[1]
Razed[2] to the ground is Eretria — but Athens,
  shall Athens sink,
Drop into dust and die — the flower of Hellas
  utterly die,
Die with the wide world spitting at Sparta, the
  stupid, the stander-by?
Answer me quick, what help, what hand do you
  stretch o'er destruction's brink?
How — when? No care for my limbs! — there's
  lightning in all and some —
Fresh and fit your message to bear, once lips give
  it birth!"

O my Athens — Sparta love thee? Did Sparta
   respond?
Every face of her leered in a furrow of envy, mistrust,
Malice, — each eye of her gave me its glitter of
   gratified hate!
Gravely they turned to take counsel, to cast for
   excuses.   I stood
Quivering, — the limbs of me fretting as fire frets,
   an inch from dry wood:
" Persia has come, Athens asks aid, and still they
   debate?
Thunder, thou Zeus!   Athene, are Spartans a quarry
   beyond
Swing of thy spear? Phoibos and Artemis, clang
   them ' Ye must'!"

No bolt launched from Olumpos![1] Lo, their
   answer at last!
"Has Persia come, — does Athens ask aid, — may
   Sparta befriend?
Nowise precipitate judgment — too weighty the
   issue at stake!
Count we no time lost time which lags thro' respect
   to the Gods!
Ponder that precept of old, ' No warfare, whatever
   the odds

In your favor, so long as the moon, half-orbed, is
    unable to take
Full-circle her state in the sky!' Already she
    rounds to it fast:
Athens must wait, patient as we — who judgment
    suspend."

Athens, — except for that sparkle, — thy name, I
    had moldered to ash!
That sent a blaze thro' my blood; off, off and away
    was I back,
— Not one word to waste, one look to lose on the
    false and the vile!
Yet "O Gods of my land!" I cried, as each hillock
    and plain,
Wood and stream, I knew, I named, rushing past
    them again,
"Have ye kept faith, proved mindful of honors we
    paid you erewhile?
Vain was the filleted [1] victim, the fulsome libation!
    Too rash
Love in its choice, paid you so largely service so
    slack!

"Oak and olive and bay,[2] — I bid you cease to en-
    wreathe

Brows made bold by your leaf! Fade at the Per-
　　sian's foot,

You that, our patrons were pledged, should never
　　adorn a slave!

Rather I hail thee, Parnes,[1] — trust to thy wild
　　waste tract!

Treeless, herbless, lifeless mountain! What mat-
　　ter if slacked

My speed may hardly be, for homage to crag and
　　to cave

No deity deigns to drape with verdure? — at least
　　I can breathe,

Fear in thee no fraud from the blind, no lie from
　　the mute!"

Such my cry as, rapid, I ran over Parnes' ridge;

Gully and gap I clambered and cleared till, sudden,
　　a bar

Jutted, a stoppage of stone against me, blocking
　　the way.

Right! for I minded the hollow to traverse, the
　　fissure across:

"Where I could enter, there I depart by! Night in
　　the fosse? [2]

Athens to aid? Tho' the dive were thro' Erebos,
　　thus I obey —

Out of the day dive, into the day as bravely arise!
    No bridge
Better!" — when — ha! what was it I came on, of
    wonders that are?

There, in the cool of a cleft, sat he — majestical Pan!
Ivy [1] drooped wanton,[2] kissed his head, moss cush-
    ioned his hoof;
All the great God was good in the eyes grave-
    kindly — the curl
Carved on the bearded cheek, amused at a mor-
    tal's awe
As, under the human trunk, the goat-thighs grand
    I saw.
"Halt, Pheidippides!" — halt I did, my brain of a
    whirl:
" Hither to me! Why pale in my presence?" he
    gracious began:
" How is it, — Athens, only in Hellas, holds me
    aloof?
" Athens, she only, rears me no fane, makes me no
    feast!
Wherefore? Than I what godship to Athens more
    helpful of old?
Aye, and still, and forever her friend! Test Pan,
    trust me!

Go, bid Athens take heart, laugh Persia to scorn,
    have faith
In the temples and tombs! Go, say to Athens,
    'The Goat-God saith:
When Persia — so much as strews not the soil —
    is cast in the sea,
Then praise Pan who fought in the ranks with your
    most and least,
Goat-thigh to greaved-thigh,[1] made one cause with
    the free and the bold!'

"Say Pan saith: 'Let this, foreshowing the place, be
    the pledge!'"
(Gay, the liberal hand held out this herbage I bear
— Fennel,[2] — I grasped it a-tremble with dew —
    whatever it bode),
"While, as for thee . . ." But enough! He was
    gone. If I ran hitherto —
Be sure that the rest of my journey, I ran no longer,
    but flew.
Parnes to Athens — earth no more, the air was my
    road;
Here am I back. Praise Pan, we stand no more on
    the razor's edge!
Pan for Athens, Pan for me! I too have a guerdon
    rare!

Then spoke Miltiades.[1] "And thee, best runner
    of Greece,
Whose limbs did duty indeed, — what gift is prom-
    ised thyself?
Tell it us straightway, — Athens the mother de-
    mands of her son!"
Rosily blushed the youth: he paused: but, lifting at
    length
His eyes from the ground, it seemed as he gathered
    the rest of his strength
Into the utterance — "Pan spoke thus: 'For what
    thou hast done
Count on a worthy reward! Henceforth be al-
    lowed thee release
From the racer's toil, no vulgar reward in praise or
    in pelf!'

"I am bold to believe, Pan means reward the most
    to my mind!
Fight I shall, with our foremost, wherever this
    fennel may grow, —
Pound — Pan helping us — Persia to dust, and, under
    the deep,
Whelm her away for ever; and then, — no Athens
    to save, —

Marry a certain maid, I know keeps faith to the
    brave, —
Hie to my house and home: and, when my children
    shall creep
Close to my knees, — recount how the God was
    awful yet kind,
Promised their sire reward to the full — rewarding
    him — so!"   ———————

Unforeseeing one!   Yes, he fought on the Marathon
    day:
So, when Persia was dust, all cried "To Akropolis![1]
Run, Pheidippides, one race more! the meed is thy
    due!
'Athens is saved, thank Pan,' go shout!"   He
    flung down his shield,
Ran like fire once more: and the space 'twixt the
    Fennel-field
And Athens was stubble again, a field which a fire
    runs through,
Till in he broke: "Rejoice, we conquer!"   Like
    wine thro' clay,
Joy in his blood bursting his heart, he died — the
    bliss!

So, to this day, when friend meets friend, the word
    of salute

Is still "Rejoice!" — his word which brought
  rejoicing indeed.
So is Pheidippides happy for ever, — the noble
  strong man
Who could race like a god, bear the face of a god,
  whom a god loved so well,
He saw the land saved he had helped to save, and
  was suffered to tell
Such tidings, yet never decline, but, gloriously as
  he began.[1]
So to end gloriously — once to shout, thereafter be
  mute:
"Athens is saved!" — Pheidippides dies in the
  shout for his meed.

MY LAST DUCHESS

FERRARA

This poem — published in *Bells and Pomegranates* — is
the first *direct* progenitor of *Andrea del Sarto* and the other
great blank-verse monologues; in it we see the form, save for
the scarcely appreciable presence of rhyme, already devel-
oped. The poem is a subtle study in the jealousy of egoism
— not a study so much as a creation; and it places before
us, as if bitten out by the etcher's acid, a typical autocrat
of the Renaissance, with his serene self-composure of selfish-
ness, quiet uncompromising cruelty, and genuine devotion to
art. The scene and the actors in this little Italian drama

stand out before us with the most natural clearness; there
is some telling touch in every line, an infinitude of cunningly
careless details, instinct with suggestion, and an appearance
through it all of simple artless ease, such as only the very
finest art can give.

THAT'S my last Duchess painted on the wall,
Looking as if she were alive.   I call
That piece a wonder, now: Frà Pandolf's [1] hands
Worked busily a day, and there she stands.
Will 't please you sit and look at her?   I said
"Frà Pandolf" by design, for never read
Strangers like you that pictured countenance,
The depth and passion of its earnest glance,
But to myself they turned (since none puts by
The curtain I have drawn for you, but I)
And seemed as they would ask me, if they durst
How such a glance came there; so, not the first
Are you to turn and ask thus.   Sir, 'twas not
Her husband's presence only, called that spot
Of joy into the Duchess' cheek: perhaps
Frà Pandolf chanced to say "Her mantle laps
Over my lady's wrist too much," or "Paint
Must never hope to reproduce the faint
Half-flush that dies along her throat:" such stuff
Was courtesy, she thought, and cause enough
For calling up that spot of joy.   She had
A heart — how shall I say? — too soon made glad,

Too easily impressed; she liked whate'er
She looked on, and her looks went everywhere.
Sir, 'twas all one! My favor at her breast,
The dropping of the daylight in the West,
The bough of cherries some officious fool
Broke in the orchard for her, the white mule
She rode with round the terrace — all and each
Would draw from her alike the approving speech,
Or blush, at least. She thanked men, — good! but
    thanked
Somehow — I know not how — as if she ranked
My gift of a nine-hundred-years-old name
With anybody's gift. Who'd stoop to blame
This sort of trifling? Even had you skill
In speech — (which I have not) — to make your
    will
Quite clear to such an one, and say, "Just this
Or that in you disgusts me; here you miss,
Or there exceed the mark" — and if she let
Herself be lessoned so, nor plainly set
Her wits to yours, forsooth, and made excuse,
— E'en then would be some stooping; and I choose
Never to stoop. Oh, sir, she smiled, no doubt,
Whene'er I passed her; but who passed without
Much the same smile? This grew; I gave com-
    mands;[1]

Then all smiles stopped together.   There she stands
As if alive.   Will 't please you rise?   We'll meet
The company below, then.   I repeat
The Count your master's known munificence
Is ample warrant that no just pretense
Of mine for dowry will be disallowed;
Though his fair daughter's self, as I avowed
At starting, is my object.   Nay, we'll go
Together down, sir.   Notice Neptune,[1] though,
Taming a sea-horse, thought a rarity,
Which Claus of Innsbruck cast in bronze for me!"

UP AT A VILLA — DOWN IN THE CITY [2]

I

HAD I but plenty of money, money enough and to
        spare,
The house for me, no doubt, were a house in the
        city-square;
Ah, such a life, such a life, as one leads at the win-
        dow there!

II

Something to see, by Bacchus, something to hear,
        at least!
There, the whole day long, one's life is a perfect
        feast;

While up at a villa one lives, I maintain it, no more
    than a beast.

III

Well, now, look at our villa! stuck like the horn of
    a bull
Just on a mountain edge as bare as the creature's
    skull,
Save a mere shag of a bush, with hardly a leaf to
    pull!
— I scratch my own, sometimes, to see if the hair's
    turned wool.

IV

But the city, oh, the city — the square with the
    houses! Why?
They are stone-faced, white as a curd, there's
    something to take the eye!
Houses in four straight lines, not a single front
    awry:
You watch who crosses and gossips, who saunters,
    who hurries by;
Green blinds, as a matter of course, to draw when
    the sun gets high;
And the shops with fanciful signs which are painted
    properly.

V

What of a villa?   Though winter be over in March
    by rights,
'Tis May, perhaps, ere the snow shall have withered
    well off the heights!
You've the brown ploughed land before, where the
    oxen steam and wheeze,
And the hills oversmoked behind, by the faint grey
    olive trees.

VI

Is it better in May, I ask you?   You've summer
    all at once;
In a day he leaps complete with a few strong April
    suns.
'Mid the sharp, short emerald wheat, scarce risen
    three fingers well,
The wild tulip, at end of its tube, blows out its
    great red bell
Like a thin clear bubble of blood for the children
    to prick and sell.

VII

Is it ever hot in the square?   There's a fountain to
    spout and splash!
In the shade it sings and springs; in the shine such
    foam bows flash

On the horses with curling fish tails, that prance
and paddle and pash
Round the lady atop in her conch — fifty gazers
do not abash,
Though all she wears is some weeds round her waist
in a sort of a sash.

VIII

All the year long in the villa, nothing to see, though
you linger,
Except yon cypress that points like death's lean
lifted forefinger;
Some think fireflies pretty, when they mix i' the
corn and mingle,
Or thrid the stinking hemp till the stalks of it
seem atingle.
Late August or early September, the stunning
cicala [1] is shrill
And the bees keep their tiresome whine round the
resinous firs on the hill.
Enough of the seasons, — I spare you the months
of the fever and chill.

IX

Ere you open your eyes in the city, the blessed
church-bells begin;

No sooner the bells leave off than the diligence [1]
    rattles in;
You get the pick of the news and it costs you never
    a pin.
By and by there's the travelling doctor gives pills,
    lets blood, draws teeth;
Or the Pulcinello [2] trumpet breaks up the market
    beneath.
At the post-office such a scene-picture, — the new
    play, piping hot! —
And a notice how only this morning three liberal
    thieves were shot.
Above it, behold the Archbishop's most fatherly
    of rebukes,
And beneath, with his crown and his lion, some
    little new law of the Duke's!
Or a sonnet with flowery marge, to the Reverend
    Don So-and-So,
Who is Dante,[3] Boccaccio, Petrarca, St. Jerome, and
    Cicero,
"And moreover" (the sonnet goes rhyming), "the
    skirts of St. Paul has reached,
Having preached us those six Lent lectures, more
    unctuous than ever he preached."
Noon strikes, — here sweeps the procession! our
    Lady borne smiling and smart

With a pink gauze gown, all spangles, and seven
swords stuck in her heart!
Bang-whang-whang goes the drum, *tootle-te-tootle* the
fife;
No keeping one's haunches still; it's the greatest
pleasure in life.

X

But bless you, it's dear, — it's dear! fowls, wine at
double the rate.
They've clapped a new tax upon salt, and what oil
pays passing the gate
It's a horror to think of. And so, the villa for me,
not the city!
Beggars can scarcely be choosers; but still — ah,
the pity, the pity!
Look, two and two go the priests, then the monks
with cowls and sandals,
And the penitents dressed in white shirts, a-holding
the yellow candles;
One, he carries a flag up straight, and another a
cross with handles,
And the Duke's guard brings up the rear, for the
better prevention of scandals!
Bang-whang-whang goes the drum, *tootle-te-tootle*
the fife.

Oh, a day in the city-square, there is no such pleas-
ure in life.

SAUL [1]

I

SAID Abner,[2] "At last thou art come! Ere I tell,
ere thou speak,

Kiss my cheek, wish me well!" Then I wished it,
and did kiss his cheek.

And he, "Since the king, O my friend, for thy
countenance sent,

Neither drunken nor eaten have we; nor until from
his tent

Thou return with the joyful assurance the King
liveth yet,

Shall our lip with the honey be bright, with the
water be wet.

For out of the black mid-tent's silence, a space of
three days,

Not a sound hath escaped to thy servants, of prayer
nor of praise,

To betoken that Saul and the Spirit [3] have ended
their strife,

And that, faint in his triumph, the monarch sinks
back upon life.

II

"Yet now my heart leaps, O beloved! God's child
  with his dew
On thy gracious gold hair, and those lilies still liv-
  ing and blue
Just broken to twine round thy harp-strings, as if
  no wild heat
Were now raging to torture the desert!"

III

Then I, as was meet,
Knelt down to the God of my fathers, and rose on
  my feet,
And ran o'er the sand burnt to powder. The tent
  was unlooped;
I pulled up the spear that obstructed, and under I
  stooped;
Hands and knees on the slippery grass-patch, all
  withered and gone,
That extends to the second inclosure, I groped my
  way on
Till I felt where the foldskirts fly open. Then once
  more I prayed,
And opened the foldskirts and entered, and was not
  afraid

But spoke, " Here is David, thy servant!" And no
  voice replied.

At the first I saw naught but the blackness; but soon
  I descried

A something more black than the blackness — the
  vast, the upright

Main prop which sustains the pavilion: and slow
  into sight

Grew a figure against it, gigantic and blackest of
  all.

Then a sunbeam, that burst thro' the tent roof,
  showed Saul.

IV

He stood as erect as that tent-prop, both arms
  stretched out wide,

On the great cross-support in the center, that goes
  to each side;

He relaxed not a muscle, but hung there as, caught
  in his pangs

And waiting his change, the king serpent all heavily
  hangs,

Far away from his kind, in the pine, till deliverance
  come

With the spring-time, — so agonized Saul, drear [1]
  and stark, blind and dumb.

V

Then I tuned my harp, — took off the lilies we
    twine round its chords
Lest they snap 'neath the stress of the noontide —
    those sunbeams like swords!
And I first played the tune all our sheep know, as,
    one after one,
So docile they come to the pen-door till folding be
    done.
They are white and untorn by the bushes, for lo,
    they have fed
Where the long grasses stifle the water within the
    stream's bed;
And now one after one seeks its lodgings, as star fol-
    lows star
Into eve and the blue far above us, — so blue and
    so far!

VI

— Then the tune, for which quails on the cornland
    will each leave his mate
To fly after the player; then, what makes the crickets
    elate
Till for boldness they fight one another: and then,
    what has weight

To set the quick jerboa [1] a-musing outside his sand
    house —
There are none such as he for a wonder, half bird
    and half mouse!
God made all the creatures and gave them our love
    and our fear,
To give sign, we and they are his children, one
    family here.

VII

Then I played the help-tune of our reapers, their
    wine-song, when hand
Grasps at hand, eye lights eye in good friendship,
    and great hearts expand
And grow one in the sense of this world's life. —
    And then, the last song
When the dead man is praised on his journey —
    "Bear him along
With his few faults shut up like dead flowerets!
    Are balm-seeds not here
To console us? The land has none left such as he
    on the bier.
Oh, would we might keep thee, my brother!" —
    And then, the glad chant
Of the marriage, — first go the young maidens,
    next, she whom we vaunt

As the beauty, the pride of our dwelling. — And
    then, the great march
Wherein man runs to man to assist him and buttress
    an arch
Naught can break; who shall harm them, our friends?
    — Then, the chorus intoned
As the Levites go up to the altar in glory enthroned.
But I stopped here: for here in the darkness Saul
    groaned.

VIII

And I paused, held my breath in such silence, and
    listened apart;
And the tent shook, for mighty Saul shuddered:
    and sparkles 'gan dart
From the jewels that woke in his turban, at once
    with a start
All its lordly male-sapphires,[1] and rubies courageous
    at heart.
So the head: but the body still moved not, still
    hung there erect.
And I bent once again to my playing, pursued it
    unchecked,
As I sang, —

IX

        "Oh, our manhood's prime vigor! No
spirit feels waste,

Not a muscle is stopped in its playing nor sinew
    unbraced.

Oh, the wild joys of living! the leaping from rock
    up to rock,

The strong rending of boughs from the fir tree, the
    cool silver shock

Of the plunge in a pool's living water, the hunt of
    the bear,

And the sultriness showing the lion is couched in
    his lair.

And the meal, the rich dates yellowed over with
    gold dust divine,

And the locust-flesh [1] steeped in the pitcher, the full
    draught of wine,

And the sleep in the dried river-channel where bul-
    rushes tell

That the water was wont to go warbling so softly
    and well.

How good is man's life, the mere living! [2] how fit
    to employ

All the heart and the soul and the senses for ever
    in joy!

Hast thou loved the white locks of thy father, whose
    sword thou didst guard

When he trusted thee forth with the armies, for
    glorious reward?

Didst thou see the thin hands of thy mother, held
    up as men sung

The low song of the nearly departed, and hear her
    faint tongue

Joining in while it could to the witness, 'Let one
    more attest,

I have lived, seen God's hand thro' a lifetime, and
    all was for best!'

Then they sung thro' their tears in strong triumph,
    not much, but the rest.

And thy brothers, the help and the contest,[1] the
    working whence grew

Such result as, from seething grape-bundles, the
    spirit strained true:

And the friends of thy boyhood — that boyhood of
    wonder and hope,

Present promise and wealth of the future beyond
    the eye's scope, —

Till lo, thou art grown to a monarch; a people is
    thine:

And all gifts, which the world offers singly, on one
    head combine!

On one head, all the beauty and strength, love and
    rage (like the throe [2]

That, a-work in the rock, helps its labor and lets
    the gold go),

High ambition and deeds which surpass it, fame
    crowning them, — all
Brought to blaze on the head of one creature —
    King Saul!" [1]

X

And lo, with that leap of my spirit, — heart, hand,
    harp, and voice,
Each lifting Saul's name out of sorrow, each bidding
    rejoice
Saul's fame in the light it was made for — as when,
    dare I say,
The Lord's army, in rapture of service, strains thro'
    its array,
And upsoareth the cherubim-chariot [2]— "Saul!"
    cried I, and stopped,
And waited the thing that should follow. Then
    Saul, who hung propped
By the tent's cross-support in the center, was
    struck by his name.
Have ye seen when Spring's arrowy summons goes
    right to the aim,
And some mountain, the last to withstand her, that
    held (he alone,
While the vale laughed in freedom and flowers) on
    a broad bust of stone

A year's snow bound about for a breastplate, —
    leaves grasp of the sheet?
Fold on fold all at once it crowds thunderously
    down to his feet,
And there fronts you, stark, black, but alive yet,
    your mountain of old,
With his rents, the successive bequeathings of ages
    untold:
Yea, each harm got in fighting your battles, each
    furrow and scar
Of his head thrust 'twixt you and the tempest —
    all hail, there they are!
— Now again to be softened with verdure, again
    hold the nest
Of the dove, tempt the goat and its young to the
    green on his crest
For their food in the ardors of summer. One long
    shudder thrilled
All the tent till the very air tingled, then sank and
    was stilled
At the King's self left standing before me, released
    and aware.
What was gone, what remained? All to traverse
    'twixt hope and despair.[1]
Death was past, life not come: so he waited. Awhile
    his right hand

Held the brow, helped the eyes left too vacant,
    forthwith to remand
To their place what new objects should enter: 'twas
    Saul as before.
I looked up, and dared gaze at those eyes, nor was
    hurt any more
Than by slow pallid sunsets in autumn, ye watch
    from the shore,
At their sad level gaze o'er the ocean — a sun's
    slow decline
Over hills which, resolved in stern silence, o'erlap
    and entwine
Base with base to knit strength more intensely: so,
    arm folded arm
O'er the chest whose slow heavings subsided.

XI

           What spell or what charm,
(For, awhile there was trouble within me) what
    next should I urge
To sustain him where song had restored him?
    Song filled to the verge
His cup with the wine of this life, pressing all that
    it yields
Of mere fruitage, the strength and the beauty:
    beyond, on what fields,

Glean a vintage more potent and perfect to brighten
    the eye,
And bring blood to the lip, and commend them the
    cup they put by?
He saith, "It is good"; still he drinks not: he lets
    me praise life,
Gives assent, yet would die for his own part.

XII

               Then fancies grew rife
Which had come long ago on the pasture, when
    round me the sheep
Fed in silence — above, the one eagle wheeled slow
    as in sleep;
And I lay in my hollow and mused on the world
    that might lie
'Neath his ken, tho' I saw but the strip 'twixt the
    hill and the sky:
And I laughed — "Since my days are ordained to
    be passed with my flocks,
Let me people at least, with my fancies, the plains
    and the rocks,
Dream the life I am never to mix with, and image
    the show
Of mankind as they live in those fashions I hardly
    shall know!

Schemes of life, its best rules and right uses, the
    courage that gains,
And the prudence that keeps what men strive for!"
    And now these old trains
Of vague thought came again; I grew surer; so,
    once more the string
Of my harp made response to my spirit, as thus —

XIII

                         " Yea, my King,"
I began — "thou dost well in rejecting mere com-
    forts that spring
From the mere mortal life held in common by man
    and by brute:
In our flesh grows the branch of this life, in our
    soul it bears fruit.
Thou hast marked the slow rise of the tree, — how
    its stem trembled first
Till it passed the kid's lip, the stag's antler; then
    safely outburst
The fan-branches all round; and thou mindest when
    these too, in turn
Broke a-bloom and the palm-tree seemed perfect·
    yet more was to learn,
E'en the good that comes in with the palm-fruit.
    Our dates shall we slight,

When their juice brings a cure for all sorrow? or
    care for the plight
Of the palm's self whose slow growth produced
    them? Not so! stem and branch
Shall decay, nor be known in their place, while the
    palm-wine shall stanch
Every wound of man's spirit in winter. I pour thee
    such wine.
Leave the flesh to the fate it was fit for! the spirit
    be thine!
By the spirit, when age shall o'ercome thee. thou
    still shalt enjoy
More indeed, than at first when, inconscious, the
    life of a boy.
Crush that life, and behold its wine running! Each
    deed thou hast done
Dies, revives, goes to work in the world; until e'en
    as the sun
Looking down on the earth, tho' clouds spoil him,
    tho' tempests efface,
Can find nothing his own deed produced not, must
    everywhere trace
The results of his past summer-prime, — so, each
    ray of thy will,
Every flash of thy passion and prowess, long over,
    shall thrill

Thy whole people, the countless, with ardor, till
    they too give forth

A like cheer to their sons: who in turn, fill tbe
    South and the North

With the radiance thy deed was the germ of. Ca-
    rouse in the past!

But the license of age has its limit; thou diest at
    last.

As the lion when age dims his eyeball, the rose at
    her height.

So with man — so his power and his beauty for ever
    take flight.

No! Again a long draught of my soul-wine! Look
    forth o'er the years!

Thou hast done now with eyes for the actual; begin
    with the seer's!

Is Saul dead? In the depth of the vale make his
    tomb — bid arise

A gray mountain of marble heaped four-square, till,
    built to the skies,

Let it mark where the great First King [1] slumbers:
    whose fame would ye know?

Up above see the rock's naked face, where the
    record shall go

In great characters cut by the scribe, — Such was
    Saul, so he did;

With the sages directing the work, by the populace
  chid, —
For not half, they'll affirm, is comprised there!
  Which fault to amend,
In the grove with his kind grows the cedar, whereon
  they shall spend
(See, in tablets 'tis level before them) their praise,
  and record
With the gold of the graver, Saul's story, — the
  statesman's great word
Side by side with the poet's sweet comment. The
  river's a-wave
With smooth paper-reeds grazing each other when
  prophet-winds rave:
So the pen gives unborn generations their due and
  their part
In thy being! Then, first of the mighty, thank
  God that thou art!"

XIV

And behold while I sang . . . but O Thou who didst
  grant me that day,
And before it not seldom has granted thy help to
  essay,
Carry on and complete an adventure, — my shield
  and my sword

In that act where my soul was thy servant, thy
    word was my word, —
Still be with me, who then at the summit of human
    endeavor
And scaling the highest, man's thought could, gazed
    hopeless as ever
On the new stretch of heaven above me — till,
    mighty to save,
Just one lift of thy hand cleared that distance —
    God's throne from man's grave!
Let me tell out my tale to its ending — my voice
    to my heart
Which can scarce dare believe in what marvels last
    night I took part,
As this morning I gather the fragments, alone with
    my sheep,
And still fear lest the terrible glory evanish [1] like
    sleep!
For I wake in the grey dewy covert, while Hebron [2]
    upheaves
The dawn struggling with night on his shoulder,
    and Kidron [3] retrieves
Slow the damage of yesterday's sunshine. [4]

XV

I say then, — my song
While I sang thus, assuring the monarch, and, ever
more strong,
Made a proffer of good to console him, — he slowly
resumed
His old motions and habitudes kingly. The right
hand replumed
His black locks to their wonted composure, adjusted
the swathes
Of his turban, and see — the huge sweat that his
countenance bathes,
He wipes off the robe; and he girds now his loins as
of yore,
And feels slow for the armlets of price, with the
clasp set before.
He is Saul, ye remember in glory, — ere error had bent
The broad brow from the daily communion; and
still, tho' much spent
Be the life and the bearing that front you, the same,
God did choose,
To receive what a man may waste, desecrate, never
quite lose.
So sank he along by the tent-prop, till, stayed by
the pile

Of his armor and war-cloak and garments, he leaned
    there awhile,
And sat out my singing, — one arm round the tent-
    prop, to raise
His bent head, and the other hung slack — till I
    touched on the praise
I foresaw from all men in all time, to the man
    patient there;
And thus ended, the harp falling forward. Then
    first I was 'ware
That he sat, as I say, with my head just above his
    vast knees
Which were thrust out on each side around me, like
    oak roots which please
To encircle a lamb when it slumbers. I looked up
    to know
If the best I could do had brought solace: he spoke
    not, but slow
Lifted up the hand slack at his side, till he laid it
    with care
Soft and grave, but in mild settled will, on my
    brow: thro' my hair
The large fingers were pushed, and he bent back
    my head, with kind power —
All my face back, intent to peruse it, as men do a
    flower.

)Thus held he me there with his great eyes that
　　scrutinized mine —
And oh, all my heart how it loved him! but where
　　was the sign?
I yearned — "Could I help thee, my father, invent-
　　ing a bliss,
I would add, to that life of the past, both the future
　　and this;
I would give thee new life altogether, as good, ages
　　hence,
As this moment, — had love but the warrant, love's
　　heart to dispense!"

XVI
Then the truth came upon me.　No harp more —
　, no song more! outbroke —[1]

XVII
"I have gone the whole round of creation: I saw
　　and I spoke;
I, a work of God's hand for that purpose, received
　　in my brain
And pronounced on the rest of his handwork —
　　returned him again
His creation's approval or censure: I spoke as I
　　saw.

Reported, as man may of God's work — all's love,(
    yet all's law.

Now I lay down the judgeship he lent me. Each
    faculty tasked

To perceive him has gained an abyss, where a dew-
    drop was asked.

Have I knowledge? confounded it shrivels at Wis-
    dom laid bare.

Have I forethought? how purblind,[1] how blank, to
    the Infinite Care!

Do I task any faculty highest, to image success?

I but open my eyes, — and perfection, no more and
    no less,

In the kind I imagined, full-fronts me, and God is
    seen God

In the star, in the stone, in the flesh, in the soul and
    the clod.

And thus looking within and around me, I ever renew

(With that stoop of the soul which in bending
    upraises it too)

The submission of man's nothing-perfect to God's
    all-complete,

As by each new obeisance in spirit, I climb to his
    feet.

Yet with all this abounding experience, this deity
    known,

I shall dare to discover some province, some gift of
 my own.
There's a faculty pleasant to exercise, hard to
 hoodwink,
I am fain to keep still in abeyance (I laugh as I
 think),
Lest, insisting to claim and parade in it, wot ye, I
 worst
E'en the Giver in one gift. — Behold, I could love
 if I durst!
But I sink the pretension as fearing a man may
 o'ertake
God's own speed in the one way of love: I abstain
 for love's sake.
— What, my soul? see thus far and no farther?
 when doors great and small,
Nine-and-ninety flew ope at our touch, should the
 hundredth appall?
In the least things have faith, yet distrust in the
 greatest of all?
Do I find love so full in my nature, God's ultimate
 gift,
That I doubt his own love can compete with it?
 Here, the parts shift?
Here, the creature surpass the creator, — the end,
 what began?

Would I fain in my impotent yearning do all for
    this man,

And dare doubt he alone shall not help him, who
    yet alone can?

Would it ever have entered my mind, the bare will,
    much less power,

To bestow on this Saul what I sang of, the mar-
    velous dower

Of the life he was gifted and filled with? to make
    such a soul,

Such a body, and then such an earth for insphering
    the whole?

And doth it not enter my mind (as my warm tears
    attest),

These good things being given, to go on, and give
    one more, the best?

Aye, to save and redeem and restore him, maintain
    at the height

This perfection, — succeed, with life's dayspring,
    death's minute of night?

Interpose at the difficult minute, snatch Saul the
    mistake,

Saul the failure, the ruin he seems now, — and bid
    him awake

From the dream, the probation, the prelude, to
    find himself set

Clear and safe in new light and new life, — a new
    harmony yet
To be run and continued, and ended — who knows?
    — or endure!
The man taught enough by life's dream, of the rest
    to make sure;
By the pain-throb, triumphantly winning intensi-
    fied bliss,
And the next world's reward and repose, by the
    struggles in this."

XVIII

"I believe it! 'Tis thou, God, that givest, 'tis I
    who receive:
In the first is the last, in thy will is my power to
    believe.
All's one gift: thou canst grant it moreover, as
    prompt to my prayer,
As I breathe out this breath, as I open these arms
    to the air.
From thy will stream the worlds, life and nature,
    thy dread Sabaoth:[1]
I will? — the mere atoms despise me! Why am I
    not loath
To look that, even that in the face too? Why is it
    I dare

Think but lightly of such impuissance? [1] What
    stops my despair?

This; — 'tis not what man Does which exalts him,
    but what man Would do! [2]

See the King — I would help him, but cannot, the
    wishes fall through.

Could I wrestle to raise him from sorrow, grow poor
    to enrich,

To fill up his life, starve my own out, I would —
    knowing which,

I know that my service is perfect. Oh, speak thro'
    me now!

Would I suffer for him that I love? So wouldst
    thou — so wilt thou!

So shall crown thee the topmost, ineffablest, utter-
    most crown —

And thy love fill infinitude wholly, nor leave up
    nor down

One spot for the creature to stand in! It is by no
    breath,

Turn of eye, wave of hand, that salvation joins
    issue with death!

As thy love is discovered almighty, almighty be
    proved

Thy power, that exists with and for it, of being
    Beloved!

He who did most, shall bear most; the strongest
    shall stand the most weak.
'Tis the weakness in strength, that I cry for! my
    flesh, that I seek
In the Godhead! I seek and I find it. O Saul, it
    shall be
A Face like my face that receives thee: a Man like
    to me,
Thou shalt love and be loved by, for ever: a Hand
    like this hand
Shall throw open the gates of new life to thee! See
    the Christ stand!"

XIX

I know not too well how I found my way home in
    the night.
There were witnesses, cohorts about me, to left and
    to right,
Angels, powers, the unuttered, unseen, the alive,
    the aware:
I repressed, I got thro' them as hardly, as strug-
    glingly there,
As a runner beset by the populace famished for
    news —
Life or death. The whole earth was awakened,
    hell loosed with her crews;

And the stars of night beat with emotion, and
    tingled and shot

Out in fire the strong pain of pent knowledge: but
    I fainted not,

For the Hand still impelled me at once and sup-
    ported, suppressed

All the tumult, and quenched it with quiet, and
    holy behest,

Till the rapture was shut in itself, and the earth
    sank to rest.

Anon at the dawn, all that trouble had withered
    from earth —

Not so much, but I saw it die out in the day's
    tender birth;

In the gathered intensity brought to the gray of
    the hills;

In the shuddering forests' held breath; in the sud-
    den wind-thrills;

In the startled wild beasts that bore off, each with
    eye sidling still,

Tho' averted with wonder and dread; in the birds
    stiff and chill

That rose heavily as I approached them, made
    stupid with awe:

E'en the serpent that slid away silent — he felt the
    new law.

The 'same stared in the white humid faces upturned
    by the flowers;
The same worked in the heart of the cedar and
    moved the vine bowers:
And the little brooks witnessing murmured, per-
    sistent and low,
With their obstinate, all but hushed voices — "E'en
    so, it is so!" [1]

A GRAMMARIAN'S FUNERAL [2]

SHORTLY AFTER THE REVIVAL OF LEARNING IN EUROPE

LET us begin and carry up this corpse,
    Singing together.
Leave we the common crofts,[3] the vulgar thorpes,
    Each in its tether [4]
Sleeping safe on the bosom of the plain,
    Cared-for till cock-crow:
Look out if yonder be not day again
    Rimming the rock-row! [5]
That's the appropriate country; there man's thought,
    Rarer, intenser,
Self-gathered for an outbreak, as it ought,
    Chafes in the censer.

Leave we the unlettered plain its herd and crop;
    Seek we sepulture
On a tall mountain, citied to the top,
    Crowded with culture!
All the peaks soar, but one the rest excels;
    Clouds overcome [1] it;
No! yonder sparkle is the citadel's
    Circling its summit.
Thither our path lies; wind we up the heights:
    Wait ye the warning?
Our low life was the level's and the night's:
    He's for the morning.
Step to a tune, square chests, erect each head,
    'Ware the beholders!
This is our master, famous, calm, and dead,
    Borne on our shoulders.

Sleep, crop and herd! sleep, darkling thorpe and
    croft
    Safe from the weather!
He, whom we convoy to his grave aloft,
    Singing together,
He was a man born with thy face and throat,
    Lyric Apollo!
Long he lived nameless: how should spring take
    note

Winter would follow?
Till lo, the little touch, and youth was gone!
   Cramped and diminished,
Moaned he, "New measures, other feet anon!
   My dance is finished!"
No, that's the world's way; (keep the mountain-side,
   Make for the city!)
He knew the signal, and stepped on with pride
   Over men's pity;
Left play for work, and grappled with the world
   Bent on escaping:
"What's in the scroll," quoth he, "thou keepest
    furled?
   Show me their shaping,
Theirs who most studied man, the bard and sage,—
   Give!" — So, he gowned him,[1]
Straight got by heart that book to its last page:
   Learned, we found him.
Yea, but we found him bald too, eyes like lead,
   Accents uncertain:
"Time to taste life," another would have said,
   "Up with the curtain!"
This man said rather, "Actual life comes next?
   Patience a moment!
Grant I have mastered learning's crabbed text,
   Still there's the comment.

Let me know all!   Prate not of most or least,
    Painful or easy!
Even to the crumbs I'd fain eat up the feast,
    Aye, nor feel queasy." [1]
Oh, such a life as he resolved to live,
    When he had learned it,
When he had gathered all books had to give!
    Sooner, he spurned it.
Image the whole, then execute the parts —
    Fancy the fabric
Quite, ere you build, ere steel strike fire from quartz,
    Ere mortar dab brick! [2]

(Here's the town-gate reached; there's the market-
    place
    Gaping before us.)
Yea, this in him was the peculiar grace
    (Hearten our chorus!)
That before living he'd learn how to live —
    No end to learning:
Earn the means first — God surely will contrive
    Use for our earning.
Others mistrust and say, "But time escapes!
    Live now or never!"
He said, "What's time?   Leave Now for dogs and
    apes!

Man has Forever."
Back to his book then: deeper drooped his head:
   Calculus [1] racked him:
Leaden before, his eyes grew dross of lead:
   Tussis attacked him.
"Now, master, take a little rest!" — not he!
   (Caution redoubled!
Step two abreast, the way winds narrowly!)
   Not a whit troubled,
Back to his studies, fresher than at first,
   Fierce as a dragon
He (soul-hydroptic [2] with a sacred thirst)
   Sucked at the flagon.
Oh, if we draw a circle premature,
   Heedless of far gain,
Greedy for quick returns of profit, sure
   Bad is our bargain!
Was it not great? did not he throw on God
   (He loves the burthen) —
God's task to make the heavenly period
   Perfect the earthen? [3]
Did not he magnify the mind, show clear
   Just what it all meant?
He would not discount life, as fools do here,
   Paid by installment.
He ventured neck or nothing — heaven's success

Found, or earth's failure:
"Wilt thou trust death or not?" He answered
    " Yes!
Hence with life's pale lure!"
That low man seeks a little thing to do,
    Sees it and does it:
This high man, with a great thing to pursue,
    Dies ere he knows it.
That low man goes on adding one to one,
    His hundred's soon hit:
This high man, aiming at a million,
    Misses an unit.
That, has the world here — should he need the next,
    Let the world mind him!
This, throws himself on God, and unperplexed
    Seeking shall find Him.[1]
So, with the throttling hands of death at strife,
    Ground he at grammar;
Still, thro' the rattle, parts of speech were rife:
    While he could stammer
He settled *Hoti's* business — let it be! —
    Properly based *Oun* —
Gave us the doctrine of the enclitic *De*,[2]
    Dead from the waist down.
Well, here's the platform, here's the proper place:
    Hail to your purlieus,[3]

All ye highfliers of the feathered race,
  Swallows and curlews!
Here's the top-peak; the multitude below
  Live, for they can, there:
This man decided not to Live but Know —
  Bury this man there?
Here — here's his place,[1] where meteors shoot,
    clouds form,
  Lightnings are loosened,
Stars come and go! Let joy break with the storm,
  Peace let the dew send!
Lofty designs must close in like effects:
  Loftily lying,
Leave him — still loftier than the world suspects,   .
  Living and dying.

SONG FROM "PIPPA PASSES"[2]

  THE year's at the spring,
  And day's at the morn;
  Morning's at seven;
  The hill-side's dew-pearled;
  The lark's on the wing;
  The snail's on the thorn;
  God's in His heaven —
  All's right with the world!

AN EPISTLE [1]

CONTAINING THE STRANGE MEDICAL EXPERIENCE OF KARSHISH, THE ARAB PHYSICIAN

KARSHISH, the picker-up of learning's crumbs,
The not-incurious in God's handiwork
(This man's-flesh he hath admirably made,
Blown like a bubble, kneaded like a paste,
To coop up and keep down on earth a space
That puff of vapor from his mouth, man's soul)
—— To Abib, all-sagacious in our art,
Breeder in me of what poor skill I boast,
Like me inquisitive how pricks and cracks
Befall the flesh thro' too much stress and strain,
Whereby the wily vapor fain would slip
Back and rejoin its source before the term, —
And aptest in contrivance (under God)
To baffle it by deftly stopping such: —
The vagrant Scholar to his sage at home
Sends greeting (health and knowledge, fame with
     peace)
Three samples of true snake-stone [2] — rarer still,
One of the other sort, the melon-shaped,
(But fitter, pounded fine, for charms than drugs)
And writeth now the twenty-second time.

My journeyings were brought [1] to Jericho:
Thus I resume.   Who studious in our art
Shall count a little labor unrepaid?
I have shed sweat enough, left flesh and bone
On many a flinty furlong of this land.
Also the country-side is all on fire
With rumors of a marching hitherward:
Some say Vespasian cometh, some, his son. [2]
A black lynx snarled and pricked a tufted ear:
Lust of my blood inflamed his yellow balls:
I cried and threw my staff and he was gone.
Twice have the robbers stripped and beaten me,
And once a town declared me for a spy; [3]
But at the end, I reach Jerusalem,
Since this poor covert where I pass the night,
This Bethany, [4] lies scarce the distance thence
A man with plague-sores at the third degree
Runs till he drops down dead.   Thou laughest here!
'Sooth, it elates me, thus reposed and safe,
To void the stuffing of my travel-scrip
And share with thee whatever Jewry yields.
A viscid choler [5] is observable
In tertians, I was nearly bold to say;
And falling-sickness hath a happier cure
Than our school wots of: there's a spider [6] here
Weaves no web, watches on the ledge of tombs,

Sprinkled with mottles on an ash-gray back;
Take five and drop them . . . but who knows his
    mind.
The Syrian run-a-gate I trust this to?
His service payeth me a sublimate
Blown up his nose to help the ailing eye.
Best wait: I reach Jerusalem at morn,
There set in order my experiences,
Gather what most deserves, and give thee all —
Or I might add, Judæa's gum-tragacanth
Scales off in purer flakes, shines clearer-grained,
Cracks 'twixt the pestle and the porphyry,[1]
In fine exceeds our produce.   Scalp-disease
Confounds me, crossing so with leprosy:
Thou hadst[2] admired one sort I gained at Zoar —
But zeal outruns discretion.   Here I end.

   Yet stay! my Syrian blinketh gratefully,
Protesteth his devotion is my price[3] —
Suppose I write what harms not, tho' he steal?
I half resolve to tell thee, yet I blush,
What set me off a-writing first of all.
An itch I had, a sting to write, a tang!
For, be it this town's barrenness — or else
The Man had something ın the look of him —
His case has struck me far more than 'tis worth.
So, pardon if — (lest presently I lose.

In the great press of novelty at hand,
The care and pains this somehow stole from me)
I bid thee take the thing while fresh in mind,
Almost in sight — for, wilt thou have the truth?
The very man is gone from me but now,
Whose ailment is the subject of discourse.
Thus then, and let thy better wit help all!

'Tis but a case of mania: subinduced
By epilepsy, at the turning point
Of trance prolonged unduly some three days
When, by the exhibition [1] of some drug
Or spell, exorcization, stroke of art
Unknown to me, and which 'twere well to know,
The evil thing, outbreaking all at once,
Left the man whole and sound of body indeed, —
But, flinging (so to speak) life's gates too wide,
Making a clear house of it too suddenly,
The first conceit that entered might inscribe
Whatever it was minded on the wall
So plainly at that vantage, as it were,
(First come, first served) that nothing subsequent
Attaineth to erase those fancy-scrawls
The just-returned and new-established soul
Hath gotten now so thoroughly by heart
That henceforth she will read or these or none.

And first — the man's own firm conviction rests
That he was dead (in fact they buried him)
— That he was dead and then restored to life
By a Nazarene physician of his tribe:
— 'Sayeth, the same bade "Rise," and he did rise.
"Such cases are diurnal," thou wilt cry.
Not so this figment! — not, that such a fume,[1]
Instead of giving way to time and health,
Should eat itself into the life of life,
As saffron tingeth flesh, blood, bones, and all!
For see, how he takes up the after-life.
The man — it is one Lazarus a Jew,
Sanguine, proportioned, fifty years of age,
The body's habit wholly laudable,
As much, indeed, beyond the common health
As he were made and put aside to show.
Think, could we penetrate by any drug
And bathe the wearied soul and worried flesh,
And bring it clear and fair, by three days' sleep!
Whence has the man the balm that brightens all?
This grown man eyes the world now like a child.
Some elders of his tribe, I should premise,
Led in their friend, obedient as a sheep,
To bear my inquisition.   While they spoke,
Now sharply, now with sorrow, — told the case, —
He listened not except I spoke to him,

But folded his two hands and let them talk,
Watching the flies that buzzed: and yet no fool.
And that's a sample how his years must go.
Look if a beggar, in fixed middle-life,
Should find a treasure, — can he use the same
With straitened habits and with tastes starved
    small,
And take at once to his impoverished brain
The sudden element that changes things,
That sets the undreamed-of rapture at his hand,
And puts the cheap old joy in the scorned dust?
Is he not such an one as moves to mirth —
Warily parsimonious, when no need,
Wasteful as drunkenness at undue times?
All prudent counsel as to what befits
The golden mean, is lost on such an one:
The man's fantastic will is the man's law.
So here — we call the treasure knowledge, say,
Increased beyond the fleshly faculty —
Heaven opened to a soul while yet on earth,
Earth forced on a soul's use while seeing heaven:
The man is witless of the size, the sum,
The value in proportion of all things,
Or whether it be little or be much.
Discourse to him of prodigious armaments
Assembled to besiege his city now,

And of the passing of a mule with gourds —
'Tis one!   Then take it on the other side,
Speak of some trifling fact, — he will gaze rapt
With stupor at its very littleness,
(Far as I see) as if in that indeed
He caught prodigious import, whole results;
And so will turn to us the bystanders
In ever the same stupor (note the point)
That we too see not with his opened eyes.
Wonder and doubt come wrongly into play,
Preposterously, at cross purposes.
Should his child sicken unto death, — why, look
For scarce abatement of his cheerfulness,
Or pretermission of the daily craft!
While a word, gesture, glance from that same child
At play or in the school or laid asleep,
Will startle him to an agony of fear,
Exasperation, just as like.   Demand
The reason why — "'tis but a word," object —
"A gesture" — he regards thee as our lord [1]
Who lived there in the pyramid alone,
Looked at us (dost thou mind?) when, being young,
We both would unadvisedly recite
Some charm's beginning, from that book of his,
Able to bid the sun throb wide and burst
All into stars, as suns grown old are wont.

Thou and the child have each a veil alike
Thrown o'er your heads, from under which ye both
Stretch your blind hands and trifle with a match
Over a mine of Greek fire,[1] did ye know!
He holds on firmly to some thread of life —
(It is the life to lead perforcedly)
Which runs across some vast distracting orb
Of glory on either side that meager thread,
Which, conscious of, he must not enter yet —
The spiritual life around the earthly life:
The law of that is known to him as this,
His heart and brain move there, his feet stay here.
So is the man perplext with impulses
Sudden to start off crosswise, not straight on,
Proclaiming what is right and wrong across,
And not along, this black thread thro' the blaze —
"It should be" balked by "here it cannot be."
And oft the man's soul springs into his face
As if he saw again and heard again
His sage that bade him "Rise" and he did rise.
Something, a word, a tick o' the blood within
Admonishes: then back he sinks at once
To ashes, who was very fire before,
In sedulous recurrence to his trade
Whereby he earneth him the daily bread;
And studiously the humbler for that pride,

Professedly the faultier that he knows
God's secret, while he holds the thread of life.
Indeed the especial marking of the man
Is prone submission to the heavenly will —
Seeing it, what it is, and why it is.
'Sayeth, he will wait patient to the last
For that same death which must restore his being
To equilibrium, body loosening soul
Divorced even now by premature full growth:
He will live, nay, it pleaseth him to live
So long as God please, and just how God please.
He even seeketh not to please God more
(Which meaneth, otherwise) than as God please.
Hence, I perceive not he affects to preach
The doctrine of his text whate'er it be,
Make proselytes as madmen thirst to do:
How can he give his neighbor the real ground,
His own conviction?   Ardent as he is —
Call his great truth a lie, why, still the old
"Be it as God please" reassureth him.
I probed the sore as thy disciples should:
"How, beast," said I, "this stolid carelessness
Sufficeth thee, when Rome is on her march
To stamp out like a little spark thy town,
Thy tribe, thy crazy tale, and thee at once?"
He merely looked with his large eyes on me.

The man is apathetic, you deduce?
Contrariwise, he loves both old and young,
Able and weak, affects the very brutes
And birds — how say I? flowers of the field —
As a wise workman recognizes tools
In a master's workshop, loving what they make.
Thus is the man as harmless as a lamb:
Only impatient, let him do his best,
At ignorance and carelessness and sin —
An indignation which is promptly curbed:
As when in certain travel I have feigned
To be an ignoramus in our art
According to some proconceived design,
And happed to hear the land's practitioners
Steeped in conceit sublimed by ignorance,
Prattle fantastically on disease,
Its cause and cure — and I must hold my peace!

Thou wilt object — Why have I not ere this
Sought out the sage himself, the Nazarene
Who wrought this cure, inquiring at the source,
Conferring with the frankness that befits?
Alas! it grieveth me, the learned leech
Perished in a tumult many years ago,
Accused, — our learning's fate, — of wizardry,
Rebellion, to the setting up a rule

And creed prodigious as described to me.
His death, which happened when the earthquake
          fell
(Prefiguring, as soon appeared, the loss
To occult learning in our lord the sage
Who lived there in the pyramid alone)
Was wrought by the mad people — that's their
          wont!
On vain recourse, as I conjecture it,
To his tried virtue, for miraculous help —
How could he stop the earthquake? That's their
          way!
The other imputations must be lies:
But take one, tho' I loathe to give it thee,
In mere respect for any good man's fame.
(And after all, our patient Lazarus
Is stark mad; should we count on what he says?
Perhaps not: tho' in writing to a leech
'Tis well to keep back nothing of a case.)
This man so cured regards the curer, then,
As — God forgive me! who but God himself,
Creator and sustainer of the world,
That came and dwelt in flesh on it awhile.
— 'Sayeth that such an one was born and lived,
Taught, healed the sick, broke bread at his own
          house,

Then died, with Lazarus by, for aught I know,
And yet was . . . what I said nor choose repeat,
And must have so avouched himself, in fact,
In hearing of this very Lazarus
Who saith — but why all this of what he saith?
Why write of trivial matters, things of price
Calling at every moment for remark?
I noticed on the margin of a pool
Blue-flowering borage,[1] the Aleppo sort,
Aboundeth, very nitrous. It is strange!

Thy pardon for this long and tedious case,
Which, now that I review it, needs must seem
Unduly dwelt upon, prolixly set forth!
Nor I myself discern in what is writ
Good cause for the peculiar interest
And awe indeed this man has touched me with.
Perhaps the journey's end, the weariness
Had wrought upon me first. I met him thus:
I crossed a ridge of short sharp broken hills
Like an old lion's cheek teeth. Out there came
A moon made like a face with certain spots
Multiform, manifold, and menacing:
Then a wind rose behind me. So we met
In this old sleepy town at unaware,
The man and I. I send thee what is writ.

Regard it as a chance, a matter risked
To this ambiguous Syrian: he may lose,
Or steal, or give it thee with equal good.
Jerusalem's repose shall make amends
For time this letter wastes, thy time and mine;
Till when, once more thy pardon and farewell![1]
The very God! think, Abib; dost thou think?
So, the All-Great, were the All-Loving too —
So, thro' the thunder comes a human voice
Saying, "O heart I made, a heart beats here!
Face, my hands fashioned, see it in myself!
Thou hast no power nor mayst conceive of mine:
But love I gave thee, with myself to love,
And thou must love me who have died for thee!"
The madman saith He said so: it is strange.[2]

MEETING AT NIGHT [3]

I

THE gray sea and the long black land;
And the yellow half-moon large and low;
And the startled little waves that leap
In fiery ringlets from their sleep,
As I gain the cove with pushing prow,
And quench its speed i' the slushy sand.

II

Then a mile of warm sea-scented beach;
Three fields to cross till a farm appears;
A tap at the pane, the quick sharp scratch
And the blue spurt of a lighted match,
And a voice less loud, thro' its joys and fears,
Than the two hearts beating each to each!

PARTING AT MORNING

ROUND the cape of a sudden came the sea,
And the sun looked over the mountain's rim:
And straight was a path of gold for him,
And the need of a world of men for me.

PROSPICE [1]

FEAR death? — to feel the fog in my throat,
  The mist in my face,
When the snows begin, and the blasts denote
  I am nearing the place,
The power of the night, the press of the storm
  The post of the foe;
Where he stands, the Arch Fear [2] in a visible form,
  Yet the strong man must go:

For the journey is done and the summit attained,
    And the barriers fall,
Tho' a battle's to fight ere the guerdon [1] be gained,
    The reward of it all.
I was ever a fighter, so — one fight more,
    The best and the last!
I would hate that death bandaged my eyes, and
      forebore,
    And bade me creep past.
No! let me taste the whole of it, fare like my peers
    The heroes of old,
Bear the brunt,[2] in a minute pay glad life's arrears
    Of pain, darkness, and cold.
For sudden the worst turns the best to the brave,
    The black minute's at end,
And the elements' rage, the fiend-voices that rave,
    Shall dwindle, shall blend,
Shall change, shall become first a peace out of pain,
    Then a light, then thy breast,
O thou soul of my soul![3]   I shall clasp thee again,
    And with God be the rest!

EPILOGUE TO "ASOLANDO" [4]

At the midnight in the silence of the sleep-time,
    When you set your fancies free,

Will they pass to where — by death, fools think,
    imprisoned —
Low he lies who once so loved you, whom you loved
    so,
             —Pity me?

Oh to love so, be so loved, yet so mistaken!
    What had I on earth to do
With the slothful, with the mawkish,[1] the unmanly?
Like the aimless, helpless, hopeless, did I drivel
           — Being — who?

One who never turned his back but marched breast
    forward,
    Never doubted clouds would break,
Never dreamed, tho' right were worsted,[2] wrong
    would triumph,
Held we fall to rise, are baffled to fight better,
           Sleep to wake.

No, at noonday in the bustle of man's work-time
    Greet the unseen with a cheer!
Bid him forward, breast and back as either should
    be,
"Strive and thrive!" cry "Speed, — fight on, fare [3]
    ever
           There as here!"

MY STAR

ALL that I know
  Of a certain star [1]
Is, it can throw
  (Like the angled spar)
Now a dart of red,
  Now a dart of blue;
Till my friends have said
  They would fain see, too,
My star that dartles the red and the blue!
Then it stops like a bird; like a flower, hangs furled:
  They must solace themselves with the Saturn
    above it.
What matter to me if their star is a world?
  Mine has opened its soul to me; therefore I love it.

RABBI BEN EZRA

In *Rabbi ben Ezra* Mr. Browning has crystallized his re
ligious philosophy into a shape of abiding beauty. It has
been called, not rashly, the noblest of modern religious
poems. Alike in substance and in form it belongs to the
highest order of meditative poetry; and it has an almost
unique quality of grave beauty, of severe restraint, of earnest
and measured enthusiasm. This is one of those poems
which can never be profitably analyzed or commented on:
it must be read. What the *Psalm of Life* is to the people
who do not think, *Rabbi ben Ezra* might and should be to
those who do; a light through the darkness — a lantern of

guidance and a beacon of hope — to the wanderers lost and
weary in the *selva selvaggia*. It is one of those poems that
mold character.

Grow old along with me!
The best is yet to be.[1]
The last of life, for which the first was made:
Our times are in His hand
Who saith, "A whole I planned,
Youth shows but half; trust God: see all, nor be
    afraid!"

Not that, amassing flowers,
Youth sighed, "Which rose make ours,
Which lily leave and then as best recall?"
Not that, admiring stars,
It yearned, "Nor Jove, nor Mars;
Mine be some figured flame which blends, trans-
    cends them all!"

Not for such hopes and fears
Annulling youth's brief years,
Do I remonstrate: folly wide the mark!
Rather I prize the doubt
Low kinds exist without,
Finished and finite clods, untroubled by a spark.

Poor vaunt of life indeed,

Were man but formed to feed
On joy, to solely seek and find and feast;
Such feasting ended, then
As sure an end to men;
Irks care the crop-full bird?   Frets doubt the maw-
    crammed beast? [1]

Rejoice we are allied
To That which doth provide
And not partake, effect and not receive!
A spark disturbs our clod;
Nearer we hold of God [2]
Who gives, than of His tribes that take, I must
    believe.

Then, welcome each rebuff
That turns earth's smoothness rough,
Each sting that bids nor sit nor stand but go!
Be our joys three-parts pain!
Strive, and hold cheap the strain;
Learn, nor account the pang; dare, never grudge
    the throe!

For thence, — a paradox
Which comforts while it mocks, —
Shall life succeed in that it seems to fail:

What I aspired to be,
And was not, comforts me:[1]
A brute I might have been, but would not sink i'
    the scale.

What is he but a brute
Whose flesh hath soul to suit,
Whose spirit works lest arms and legs want play?
To man, propose this test —
Thy body at its best,
How far can that project thy soul on its lone
    way?

Yet gifts should prove their use:
I own the Past profuse
Of power each side, perfection every turn:
Eyes, ears took in their dole,[2]
Brain treasured up the whole;
Should not the heart beat once "How good to live
    and learn"?

Not once beat "Praise be Thine!
I see the whole design,
I, who saw Power, see now Love perfect too:
Perfect I call Thy plan:
Thanks that I was a man!

Maker, remake, complete, — I trust what Thou
    shalt do!"

For pleasant is this flesh;
Our soul, in its rose-mesh
Pulled ever to the earth, still yearns for rest:
Would we some prize might hold
To match those manifold
Possessions of the brute, — gain most, as we did
    best!

Let us not always say
"Spite of this flesh to-day
I strove, made head, gained ground upon the
    whole!"
As the bird wings and sings,
Let us cry, "All good things
Are ours, nor soul helps flesh more, now, than flesh
    helps soul!"

Therefore I summon age
To grant youth's heritage,
Life's struggle having so far reached its term:[1]
Thence shall I pass, approved
A man, for aye removed
From the developed brute; a God though in the germ.

And I shall thereupon
Take rest, ere I be gone
Once more on my adventure brave and new:
Fearless and unperplexed,
When I wage battle next,
What weapons to select, what armor to indue.

Youth ended, I shall try
My gain or loss thereby;
Leave the fire ashes, what survives is gold:
And I shall weigh the same,
Give life its praise or blame:
Young, all lay in dispute; I shall know, being old.

For, note when evening shuts,
A certain moment cuts
The deed off, calls the glory from the gray:
A whisper from the west
Shoots — "Add this to the rest,
Take it and try its worth: here dies another day."

So, still within this life,
Though lifted o'er its strife,
Let me discern, compare, pronounce at last,
"This rage was right i' the main,
That acquiescence vain:

The Future I may face now I have proved the
    Past."

For more is not reserved
To man, with soul just nerved
To act to-morrow what he learns to-day:
Here, work enough to watch
The Master work, and catch
Hints of the proper craft, tricks of the tool's true
    play.

As it was better, youth
Should strive, through acts uncouth,
Toward making, than repose on aught found made:
So, better, age, exempt
From strife, should know, than tempt
Further. Thou waitedst age: wait death, nor be
    afraid!

Enough now, if the Right
And Good and Infinite
Be named here, as thou callest thy hand thine own,
With knowledge absolute,
Subject to no dispute
From fools that crowded youth, nor let thee feel
    alone.

Be there, for once and all,
Severed great minds from small,
Announced to each his station in the Past!
Was I, the world arraigned,
Were they, my soul disdained,
Right? [1] Let age speak the truth and give us
    peace at last!

Now, who shall arbitrate?
Ten men love what I hate,
Shun what I follow, slight what I receive;
Ten, who in ears and eyes
Match me: we all surmise,
They, this thing, and I, that: whom shall my soul
    believe?

Not on the vulgar mass
Called "work," must sentence pass,
Things done, that took the eye and had the price,
O'er which, from level stand,
The low world laid its hand,
Found straightway to its mind, could value in a
    trice:

But all, the world's coarse thumb
And finger failed to plumb,

So passed in making up the main account:
All instincts immature,
All purposes unsure,
That weighed not as his work, yet swelled the man's
    amount:

Thoughts hardly to be packed
Into a narrow act,
Fancies that broke through language and escaped:
All I could never be,
All men ignored in me,
This I was worth to God, whose wheel the pitcher
    shaped.

Ay, note that Potter's wheel,
That metaphor![1] and feel
Why time spins fast, why passive lies our clay, —
Thou, to whom fools propound,
When the wine makes its round,
"Since life fleets, all is change; the Past gone,
    seize to-day!"

Fool! All that is, at all,
Lasts ever, past recall;
Earth changes, but thy soul and God stand sure:
What entered into thee,

That was, is, and shall be:
Time's wheel runs back or stops: Potter and clay
    endure.

He fixed thee mid this dance
Of plastic circumstance,
This Present, thou, forsooth, wouldst fain arrest:
Machinery just meant
To give thy soul its bent,
Try thee, and turn thee forth sufficiently impressed.

What though the earlier grooves
Which ran the laughing loves
Around thy base, no longer pause and press?
What though, about thy rim,
Skull-things in order grim
Grow out, in graver mood, obey the sterner stress?

Look not thou down but up!
To uses of a cup,
The festal board, lamp's flash, and trumpet's peal,
The new wine's foaming flow,
The Master's lips aglow!
Thou, heaven's consummate cup, what needst thou
    with earth's wheel?

But I need, now as then,

Thee, God, who moldest men!

And since, not even while the whirl was worst,

Did I, — to the wheel of life

With shapes and colors rife,

Bound dizzily, — mistake my end, to slake Thy thirst

So, take and use Thy work,

Amend what flaws may lurk,

What strain o' the stuff, what warpings past the
aim!

My times be in Thy hand!

Perfect the cup as planned!

Let age approve of youth, and death complete the
same!

MEMORABILIA

This poem, says Mrs. Orr, "is a picturesque comment on
the power of personal association to give importance to any
incident, however trifling; and tends to show that, from this
point of view, no incident is more trifling than another."
The enthusiastic lover of Shelley has so idealized the poet
that he can hardly believe him to be a man that can be
spoken to like other men. For him a falling eagle-feather,
with its sudden suggestion of the ethereal poet, is enough
to drive away all other memories of the moor.

Ah, did you once see Shelley plain,

And did he stop and speak to you,

And did you speak to him again?
    How strange it seems, and new!

But you were living before that,
    And also you are living after;
And the memory I started at —
    My starting moves your laughter!

I crossed a moor, with a name of its own
    And a certain use in the world, no doubt,
Yet a hand's-breadth of it shines alone
    'Mid the blank miles round about:

For there I picked up on the heather
    And there I put inside my breast
A moulted feather, an eagle-feather!
    Well, I forget the rest.

ABT VOGLER

(AFTER HE HAS BEEN EXTEMPORIZING UPON THE
MUSICAL INSTRUMENT OF HIS INVENTION)

Abt Vogler [1] is an utterance on music which exceeds every
attempt that has ever been made in verse to set forth the
secret of the most sacred and illusive of the arts. Only the
wonderful lines in the *Merchant of Venice* come anywhere
near it. It is the richest, deepest, fullest poem on music in
the language. The wonder and beauty of it grow on one,
as the wonder and beauty of a sky, of the sea, of a landscape,

beautiful indeed and wonderful from the first, become momen-
tarily more evident, intense and absorbing. Life, religion,
and music — the *Ganzen, Guten, Schönen* of existence — are
combined in threefold unity, apprehended and interpreted
in their essential spirit.

WOULD that the structure brave, the manifold
music I build,
Bidding my organ obey, calling its keys to their
work,
Claiming each slave of the sound, at a touch, as
when Solomon willed [1]
Armies of angels that soar, legions of demons
that lurk,
Man, brute, reptile, fly, — alien of end and of aim,
Adverse, each from the other heaven-high, hell-
deep removed, —
Should rush into sight at once as he named the in-
effable Name,
And pile him a palace straight, to pleasure the
princess he loved!

Would it might tarry like his, the beautiful build-
ing of mine,
This which my keys in a crowd pressed and im-
portuned to raise!
Ah, one and all, how they helped, would dispart
now and now combine,

Zealous to hasten the work, heighten their mas-
ter his praise!
And one would bury his brow with a blind plunge
down to hell,
Burrow a while and build, broad on the roots of
things,
Then up again swim into sight, having based me
my palace well,
Founded it, fearless of flame, flat on the nether
springs.

And another would mount and march, like the
excellent minion he was,
Ay, another and yet another, one crowd but with
many a crest,
Raising my rampired walls of gold as transparent
as glass,
Eager to do and die, yield each his place to the
rest:
For higher still and higher (as a runner tips with fire,
When a great illumination surprises a festal
night —
Outlining round and round Rome's dome from
space to spire)
Up, the pinnacled glory reached, and the pride of
my soul was in sight.

In sight? Not half! for it seemed, it was certain,
　　to match man's birth,
Nature in turn conceived, obeying an impulse as I;
And the emulous heaven yearned down, made effort
　　to reach the earth,
　　As the earth had done her best, in my passion,
　　to scale the sky:
Novel splendors burst forth, grew familiar and
　　dwelt with mine,
　　Not a point nor peak but found, but fixed its
　　wandering star;
Meteor-moons, balls of blaze: and they did not pale
　　nor pine,
　　For earth had attained to heaven, there was no
　　more near nor far.

Nay more; for there wanted not who walked in the
　　glare and glow,
　　Presences plain in the place; or, fresh from the
　　Protoplast,[1]
Furnished for ages to come, when a kindlier wind
　　should blow,
　　Lured to now begin and live, in a house to their
　　liking at last;
Or else the wonderful Dead who have passed
　　through the body and gone,

But were back once more to breathe in an old
 world worth their new:
What never had been, was now; what was, as it
 shall be anon;
And what is, — shall I say, matched both? for I
 was made perfect too.[1]

All through my keys that gave their sounds to a
 wish of my soul,
 All through my soul that praised as its wish
  flowed visibly forth,
All through music and me! For think, had I
 painted the whole,
 Why, there it had stood, to see, nor the process
  so wonder-worth.
Had I written the same, made verse — still, effect
 proceeds from cause,
 Ye know why the forms are fair, ye hear how the
  tale is told;
It is all triumphant art, but art in obedience to
 laws,
 Painter and poet are proud, in the artist-list
  enrolled: —

But here is the finger of God,[2] a flash of the will
 that can,

Existent behind all laws: that made them, and,
   lo, they are!
And I know not if, save in this, such gift be allowed
   to man,
   That out of three sounds he frame, not a fourth
   sound, but a star.
Consider it well: each tone of our scale in itself is
   naught;
   It is everywhere in the world — loud, soft, and
   all is said:
Give it to me to use! I mix it with two in my
   thought,
   And, there! Ye have heard and seen: consider
   and bow the head!

Well, it is gone at last, the palace of music I
   reared;
   Gone! and the good tears start, the praises that
   come too slow;
For one is assured at first, one scarce can say that
   he feared,
   That he even gave it a thought, the gone thing
   was to go.
Never to be again! But many more of the kind
   As good, nay, better perchance: is this your com-
   fort to me?

To me, who must be saved because I cling with my
  mind
  To the same, same self, same love, same God: ay,
  what was, shall be.

Therefore to whom turn I but to thee, the ineffable
  Name?
  Builder and maker, thou, of houses not made
  with hands!
What, have fear of change from thee who art ever
  the same?
  Doubt that thy power can fill the heart that thy
  power expands?
There shall never be one lost good! What was,
  shall live as before;
  The evil is null, is naught, is silence implying
  sound;
What was good, shall be good, with, for evil, so
  much good more;
  On the earth the broken arcs; in the heaven, a
  perfect round.

All we have willed or hoped or dreamed of good,
  shall exist;
  Not its semblance, but itself; no beauty, nor good,
  nor power

Whose voice has gone forth, but each survives for
the melodist,
When eternity affirms the conception of an hour.
The high that proved too high, the heroic for earth
too hard,
The passion that left the ground to lose itself in
the sky,
Are music sent up to God by the lover and the bard;
Enough that he heard it once: we shall hear it
by-and-by.

And what is our failure here but a triumph's evi-
dence
For the fullness of the days? Have we withered
or agonized?
Why else was the pause prolonged but that sing-
ing might issue thence?
Why rushed the discords in, but that harmony
should be prized?
Sorrow is hard to bear, and doubt is slow to clear,
Each sufferer says his say, his scheme of the weal
and woe:
But God has a few of us whom he whispers in the
ear;
The rest may reason and welcome; 'tis we musi-
cians know.

Well, it is earth with me; silence resumes her reign:
  I will be patient and proud, and soberly ac-
    quiesce.
Give me the keys. I feel for the common chord
    again,
  Sliding by semitones, till I sink to the minor, —
    yes,
And I blunt it into a ninth, and I stand on alien
    ground,
  Surveying a while the heights I rolled from into
    the deep;
Which, hark, I have dared and done, for my rest-
    ing-place is found,
  The C Major of this life: so, now I will try to
    sleep.

ANDREA DEL SARTO

[CALLED "THE FAULTLESS PAINTER"]

Andrea del Sarto is a "translation into song" of the picture
called "Andrea del Sarto and his Wife," now in the Pitti
Palace, Florence. It is a perfect re-creation of the Andrea
described by Vasari, whose story is one of the saddest in the
records of art. The story is well known; how the painter,
who at one time seemed as if he might have competed with
Raphael, was ruined, as artist and as man, by his beautiful
soulless wife, the fatal Lucrezia del Fede; and how, led and
lured by her, he outraged his conscience, lowered his ideal,
and, losing all heart and hope. sank into the cold correctness,

the unerring fluency, the uniform, melancholy repetition
of a single type — his wife's — which distinguish his later
works. Mr. Browning has taken his facts from Vasari, and
he has taken them quite literally. But what a change,
what a transformation and transfiguration! No more abso-
lutely creative work has been done in our days; few more
beautiful and pathetic poems written. The mood of sad,
wistful, hopeless mournfulness of resignation which the poem
expresses is a somewhat rare one with Mr. Browning's
vivid and vivacious genius. It is an autumn twilight piece.
The very movement of the lines, their very tone and touch,
contribute to the effect. A single clear impression is made
to result from an infinity of the minutest and scarcely appre-
ciable touches: how fine these touches are, how clear the
impression, can only be hinted at in words, can be realized
only by a loving and scrupulous study.

BUT do not let us quarrel any more,
No, my Lucrezia! bear with me for once:
Sit down and all shall happen as you wish.
You turn your face, but does it bring your heart?
I'll work then for your friend's friend, never fear,
Treat his own subject after his own way,
Fix his own time, accept too his own price,
And shut the money into this small hand
When next it takes mine.   Will it? tenderly?
Oh, I'll content him, — but to-morrow, Love!
I often am much wearier than you think,
This evening more than usual: and it seems
As if — forgive now — should you let me sit
Here by the window, with your hand in mine,

And look a half hour forth on Fiesole,[1]
Both of one mind, as married people use,[2]
Quietly, quietly the evening through,
I might get up to-morrow to my work
Cheerful and fresh as ever.   Let us try.
To-morrow, how you shall be glad for this!
Your soft hand is a woman of itself,
And mine, the man's bared breast she curls inside.
Don't count the time lost, neither; you must serve
For each of the five pictures we require:
It saves a model.   So! keep looking so —
My serpentining beauty, rounds on rounds!
— How could you ever prick those perfect ears,
Even to put the pearl there! oh, so sweet —
My face, my moon, my everybody's moon,
Which everybody looks on and calls his,
And, I suppose, is looked on by in turn,
While she looks — no one's: very dear, no less.
You smile? why there's my picture ready made,
There's what we painters call our harmony!
A common grayness silvers every thing, —
All in a twilight, you and I alike
— You, at the point of your first pride in me
(That's gone, you know) — but I, at every point;
My youth, my hope, my art, being all toned down
To yonder sober pleasant Fiesole.

There's the bell clinking from the chapel-top;
That length of convent-wall across the way
Holds the trees safer, huddled more inside;
The last monk leaves the garden; days decrease,
And autumn grows, autumn in every thing.
Eh? the whole seems to fall into a shape,
As if I saw alike my work and self
And all that I was born to be and do,
A twilight-piece.   Love, we are in God's hand.
How strange now looks the life he makes us lead;
So free we seem, so fettered fast we are!
I feel he laid the fetter: let it lie!
This chamber, for example — turn your head —
All that's behind us!   You don't understand
Nor care to understand about my art,
But you can hear at least when people speak:
And that cartoon, the second from the door
— It is the thing, Love! so such things should be:
Behold Madonna! — I am bold to say.
I can do with my pencil what I know,
What I see, what at bottom of my heart
I wish for, if I ever wish so deep —
Do easily, too — when I say, perfectly.
I do not boast, perhaps: yourself are judge,
Who listened to the Legate's talk last week;
And just as much they used to say in France.[1]

At any rate 'tis easy, all of it!
No sketches first, no studies, that's long past:
I do what many dream of, all their lives,
— Dream? strive to do, and agonize to do,
And fail in doing. I could count twenty such
On twice your fingers, and not leave this town,
Who strive — you don't know how the others
    strive
To paint a little thing like that you smeared
Carelessly passing with your robes afloat, —
Yet do much less, so much less, Someone says,
(I know his name, no matter) — so much less!
Well, less is more, Lucrezia: I am judged.
There burns a truer light of God in them,
In their vexed beating stuffed and stopped-up
    brain,
Heart, or whate'er else, than goes on to prompt
This low-pulsed forthright craftsman's hand [1] of
    mine.
Their works drop groundward, but themselves, I
    know,
Reach many a time a heaven that's shut to me,
Enter and take their place there sure enough,
Though they come back and cannot tell the world.
My works are nearer heaven, but I sit here.
The sudden blood of these men! at a word —

Praise them, it boils, or blame them, it boils too.
I, painting from myself and to myself,
Know what I do, am unmoved by men's blame
Or their praise either. Somebody remarks
Morello's [1] outline there is wrongly traced,
His hue mistaken; what of that? or else,
Rightly traced and well ordered; what of that?
Speak as they please, what does the mountain
    care? [2]
Ah, but a man's reach should exceed his grasp, [3]
Or what's a heaven for?   All is silver-gray,
Placid and perfect with my art: the worse!
I know both what I want and what might gain;
And yet how profitless to know, to sigh
"Had I been two, another and myself,
Our head would have o'erlooked the world!"   No
    doubt.
Yonder's a work now, of that famous youth
The Urbinate [4] who died five years ago.
('Tis copied, George Vasari [5] sent it me.)
Well, I can fancy how he did it all,
Pouring his soul, with kings and popes to see,
Reaching, that heaven might so replenish him,
Above and through his art — for it gives way:
That arm is wrongly put — and there again—
A fault to pardon in the drawing's lines,

Its body, so to speak: its soul is right,
He means right — that, a child may understand.
Still, what an arm! and I could alter it:
But all the play, the insight and the stretch —
Out of me, out of me!   And wherefore out?
Had you enjoined them on me, given me soul,
We might have risen to Rafael, I and you.
Nay, Love, you did give all I asked, I think —
More than I merit, yes, by many times.
But had you — oh, with the same perfect brow,
And perfect eyes, and more than perfect mouth,
And the low voice my soul hears, as a bird
The fowler's pipe, and follows to the snare —
Had you, with these the same, but brought a mind!   '
Some women do so.   Had the mouth there urged
"God and the glory! never care for gain.
The present by the future,[1] what is that?
Live for fame, side by side with Agnolo![2]
Rafael is waiting: up to God, all three!"
I might have done it for you.   So it seems:
Perhaps not.   All is as God overrules.
Beside, incentives come from the soul's self;
The rest avail not.   Why do I need you?
What wife had Rafael, or has Agnolo?
In this world, who can do a thing, will not;
And who would do it, cannot, I perceive:

Yet the will's somewhat — somewhat, too, the
    power —
And thus we half-men struggle.   At the end,
God, I conclude, compensates, punishes.
'Tis safer for me, if the award be strict,
That I am something underrated here,
Poor this long while, despised, to speak the truth.
I dared not, do you know, leave home all day,
For fear of chancing on the Paris lords.[1]
The best is when they pass and look aside;
But they speak sometimes; I must bear it all.
Well may they speak!   That Francis, that first
    time,
And that long festal year at Fontainebleau!
I surely then could sometimes leave the ground,
Put on the glory, Rafael's daily wear,
In that humane great monarch's golden look, —
One finger in his beard or twisted curl
Over his mouth's good mark that made the smile,
One arm about my shoulder, round my neck,
The jingle of his gold chain in my ear,
I painting proudly with his breath on me,
All his court round him, seeing with his eyes,
Such frank French eyes, and such a fire of souls
Profuse, my hand kept plying by those hearts, —
And, best of all, this, this, this face beyond,

This in the background, waiting on my work,
To crown the issue with a last reward!
A good time, was it not, my kingly days?
And had you not grown restless . . . but I know —
'Tis done and past; 'twas right, my instinct said;
Too live the life grew, golden and not gray:
And I'm the weak-eyed bat no sun should tempt
Out of the grange whose four walls make this
    world.
How could it end in any other way?
You called me, and I came home to your heart.
The triumph was, to have ended there; then, if
I reached it ere the triumph, what is lost? [1]
Let my hands frame your face in your hair's gold,
You beautiful Lucrezia that are mine!
"Rafael did this, Andrea painted that;
The Roman's is the better when you pray,
But still the other's Virgin was his wife" [2] —
Men will excuse me. I am glad to judge
Both pictures in your presence; clearer grows
My better fortune, I resolve to think.
For, do you know, Lucrezia, as God lives,
Said one day Agnolo, his very self,
To Rafael . . . I have known it all these years . . .
(When the young man was flaming out his thoughts
Upon a palace-wall for Rome to see,

Too lifted up in heart because of it)
"Friend, there's a certain sorry little scrub
Goes up and down our Florence, none cares how,
Who, were he set to plan and execute
As you are, pricked on by your popes and kings,
Would bring the sweat into that brow of yours!"
To Rafael's! — And indeed the arm is wrong.
I hardly dare . . . yet, only you to see,
Give the chalk here — quick, thus the line should
    go!
Ay, but the soul! he's Rafael! rub it out!
Still, all I care for, if he spoke the truth,
(What he? why, who but Michel Agnolo?
Do you forget already words like those?)
If really there was such a chance so lost, —
Is, whether you're — not grateful — but more pleased.
Well, let me think so.   And you smile indeed!
This hour has been an hour!   Another smile?
If you would sit thus by me every night
I should work better, do you comprehend?
I mean that I should earn more, give you more.
See, it is settled dusk now; there's a star;
Morello's gone, the watch-lights show the wall,
The cue-owls speak the name we call them by.
Come from the window, Love, — come in, at last,
Inside the melancholy little house

We built to be so gay with. God is just.
King Francis may forgive me: oft at nights
When I look up from painting, eyes tired out,
The walls become illumined, brick from brick
Distinct, instead of mortar, fierce bright gold,
That gold of his I did cement them with!
Let us but love each other. Must you go?
That cousin here again? he waits outside?
Must see you — you, and not with me? Those
    loans?
More gaming debts to pay? you smiled for that?
Well, let smiles buy me! have you more to spend?
While hand and eye and something of a heart
Are left me, work's my ware, and what's it worth?
I'll pay my fancy. Only let me sit
The gray remainder of the evening out,
Idle, you call it, and muse perfectly
How I could paint, were I but back in France,
One picture, just one more — the Virgin's face,
Not yours this time! I want you at my side
To hear them — that is, Michel Agnolo —
Judge all I do and tell you of its worth.
Will you? To-morrow, satisfy your friend.
I take the subjects for his corridor,
Finish the portrait out of hand — there, there,
And throw him in another thing or two

If he demurs; the whole should prove enough
To pay for this same cousin's freak. Beside,
What's better and what's all I care about,
Get you the thirteen scudi for the ruff!
Love, does that please you? Ah, but what does he,
The cousin! what does he to please you more?

   I am grown peaceful as old age to-night.
I regret little, I would change still less.
Since there my past life lies, why alter it?
The very wrong to Francis! — it is true
I took his coin, was tempted and complied,
And built this house and sinned, and all is said.
My father and my mother died of want.
Well, had I riches of my own? you see
How one gets rich! Let each one bear his lot.
They were born poor, lived poor, and poor they
     died:
And I have labored somewhat in my time
And not been paid profusely. Some good son
Paint my two hundred pictures — let him try!
No doubt, there's something strikes a balance. Yes,
You love me quite enough, it seems to-night.
This must suffice me here. What would one
     have?
In heaven, perhaps, new chances, one more chance —

Four great walls in the New Jerusalem,
Meted on each side by the angel's reed,
For Leonard,[1] Rafael, Agnolo, and me
To cover — the three first without a wife,
While I have mine! So — still they overcome
Because there's still Lucrezia, — as I choose.

Again the cousin's whistle! Go, my Love

BY THE FIRESIDE

How well I know what I mean to do
  When the long, dark autumn evenings come;
And where, my soul, is [2] thy pleasant hue?
  With the music of all thy voices, dumb
In life's November too!

I shall be found by the fire, suppose,
  O'er a great wise book, as beseemeth age;
While the shutters flap as the cross-wind blows,
  And I turn the page, and I turn the page,
Not verse now, only prose!

Till the young ones whisper, finger on lip,
  "There he is at it, deep in Greek:

Now then, or never, out we slip
   To cut from the hazels by the creek
A mainmast for our ship!"

I shall be at it indeed, my friends!
   Greek puts already on either side
Such a branch-work forth as soon extends
   To a vista opening far and wide,
And I pass out where it ends.

The outside frame, like your hazel-trees —
   But the inside-archway widens fast,
And a rarer sort succeeds to these,
   And we slope to Italy at last
And youth, by green degrees.

I follow wherever I am led,
   Knowing so well the leader's hand:
Oh woman-country, wooed not wed,
   Loved all the more by earth's male-lands,
Laid to their hearts instead!

Look at the ruined chapel again
   Half-way up in the Alpine gorge!
Is that a tower, I point you plain,
   Or is it a mill, or an iron forge
Breaks solitude in vain?

A turn, and we stand in the heart of things;
  The woods are round us, heaped and dim;
From slab to slab how it slips and springs,
  The thread of water single and slim,
Through the ravage some torrent brings!

Does it feed the little lake below?
  That speck of white just on its marge
Is Pella; see, in the evening glow,
  How sharp the silver spear-heads charge
When Alp meets heaven in snow!

On our other side is the straight-up rock;
  And a path is kept 'twixt the gorge and it
By bowlder-stones, where lichens mock
  The marks on a moth, and small ferns fit
Their teeth to the polished block.

Oh the sense of the yellow mountain-flowers,
  And thorny balls, each three in one,
The chestnuts throw on our path in showers!
  For the drop of the woodlands fruit's begun,
These early November hours,

That crimson the creeper's leaf across
  Like a splash of blood, intense, abrupt,

O'er a shield else gold from rim to boss,
　　And lay it for show on the fairy-cupped
Elf-needled mat of moss,

By the rose-flesh mushrooms, undivulged
　　Last evening — nay, in to-day's first dew
Yon sudden coral nipple bulged,
　　Where a freaked fawn-colored flaky crew
Of toad-stools peep indulged.

And yonder, at foot of the fronting ridge
　　That takes the turn to a range beyond,
Is the chapel reached by the one-arched bridge,
　　Where the water is stopped in a stagnant pond
Danced over by the midge.

The chapel and bridge are of stone alike,
　　Blackish-gray and mostly wet;
Cut hemp-stalks steep [1] in the narrow dike.
　　See here again, how the lichens fret [2]
And the roots of the ivy strike!

Poor little place, where its one priest comes
　　On a festa-day, if he comes at all,
To the dozen folk from their scattered homes,
　　Gathered within that precinct small
By the dozen ways one roams —

To drop from the charcoal-burners' huts,
  Or climb from the hemp-dressers' low shed,
Leave the grange where the woodman stores his nuts,
  Or the wattled cote where the fowlers spread
Their gear on the rock's bare juts.

It has some pretension, too, this front,
  With its bit of fresco half-moon-wise
Set over the porch, Art's early wont:
  'Tis John in the Desert, I surmise,
But has borne the weather's brunt —

Not from the fault of the builder, though,
  For a pent-house properly projects
Where three carved beams make a certain show,
  Dating — good thought of our architect's —
'Five, six, nine, he lets you know.

And all day long a bird sings there,
  And a stray sheep drinks at the pond at times;
The place is silent and aware; [1]
  It has had its scenes, its joys and crimes,
But that is its own affair.

My perfect wife, my Leonor, [2]
  Oh heart, my own, oh eyes, mine too,

Whom else could I dare look backward for,
    With whom beside should I dare pursue
The path gray heads abhor?

For it leads to a crag's sheer edge with them;
    Youth, flowery all the way, there stops —
Not they; age threatens and they contemn,
    Till they reach the gulf wherein youth drops,
One inch from our life's safe hem!

With me, youth led . . . I will speak now,
    No longer watch you as you sit
Reading by firelight, that great brow
    And the spirit-small hand propping it,
Mutely, my heart knows how —

When, if I think but deep enough,
    You are wont to answer, prompt as rhyme;
And you, too, find without rebuff
    Response your soul seeks many a time,
Piercing its fine flesh-stuff.

My own, confirm me!   If I tread
    This path back, is it not in pride
To think how little I dreamed it led
    To an age so blest that, by its side,
Youth seems the waste instead?

My own, see where the years conduct!
   At first, 'twas something our two souls
Should mix as mists do; each is sucked
   In each now; on, the new stream rolls,
Whatever rocks obstruct.

Think, when our one soul understands
   The great Word which makes all things new,
When earth breaks up and heaven expands,
   How will the change strike me and you
In the house not made with hands?

Oh I must feel your brain prompt mine,
   Your heart anticipate my heart,
You must be just before, in fine, .
   See and make me see, for your part,
New depths of the divine!

But who could have expected this
   When we two drew together first
Just for the obvious human bliss,
   To satisfy life's daily thirst
With a thing men seldom miss?

Come back with me to the first of all,
   Let us lean and love it over again,

Let us now forget and now recall,
　Break the rosary in a pearly rain,
And gather what we let fall!

What did I say? [1] — that a small bird sings
　All day long, save when a brown pair
Of hawks from the wood float with wide wings
　Strained to a bell: 'gainst noonday glare
You count the streaks and rings.

But at afternoon or almost eve
　'Tis better; then the silence grows
To that degree, you half believe
　It must get rid of what it knows,
Its bosom does so heave.

Hither we walked then, side by side,
　Arm in arm and cheek to cheek,
And still I questioned or replied,
　While my heart, convulsed to really speak,
Lay choking in its pride.

Silent the crumbling bridge we cross,
　And pity and praise the chapel sweet,
And care about the fresco's loss,
　And wish for our souls a like retreat,
And wonder at the moss.

Stoop and kneel on the settle under,
  Look through the window's grated square:
Nothing to see! For fear of plunder,
  The cross is down and the altar bare,
As if thieves don't fear thunder.

We stoop and look in through the grate,
  See the little porch and rustic door,
Read duly the dead builder's date;
  Then cross the bridge that we crossed before,
Take the path again — but wait!

Oh moment one and infinite!
  The water slips o'er stock and stone;
The West is tender, hardly bright:
  How gray at once is the evening grown —
One star, its chrysolite! [1]

'We two stood there with never a third,
  But each by each, as each knew well:
The sights we saw and the sounds we heard,
  The lights and the shades made up a spell
Till the trouble grew and stirred.

Oh, the little more, and how much it is!
  And the little less, and what worlds away!

How a sound shall quicken content to bliss,
  Or a breath suspend the blood's best play,
And life be a proof of this!

Had she willed it, still had stood the screen
  So slight, so sure, 'twixt my love and her:
I could fix her face with a guard between,
  And find her soul as when friends confer,
Friends — lovers that might have been.

For my heart had a touch of the woodland time,
  Wanting to sleep now over its best.
Shake the whole tree in the summer-prime,
  But bring to the last leaf no such test!
"Hold the last fast!" runs the rhyme.

For a chance to make your little much,
  To gain a lover and lose a friend,
Venture the tree and a myriad such,
  When nothing you mar but the year can mend:
But a last leaf — fear to touch!

Yet should it unfasten itself and fall
  Eddying down till it find your face
At some slight wind — best chance of all!
  Be your heart henceforth its dwelling-place
You trembled to forestall!

Worth how well, those dark gray eyes,
   That hair so dark and dear, how worth
That a man should strive and agonize,
   And taste a veriest hell on earth
For the hope of such a prize!

You might have turned and tried a man,
   Set him a space to weary and wear,
And prove which suited more your plan,
   His best of hope or his worst despair,
Yet end as he began.

But you spared me this, like the heart you are,
   And filled my empty heart at a word.
If two lives join, there is oft a scar,
   They are one and one, with a shadowy third;
One near one is too far.

A moment after, and hands unseen
   Were hanging the night around us fast;
But we knew that a bar was broken between
   Life and life: we were mixed at last
In spite of the mortal screen.

The forests had done it; there they stood;
   We caught for a moment the powers at play:

They had mingled us so, for once and good,
   Their work was done — we might go or stay,
They relapsed to their ancient mood.

How the world is made for each of us!
   How all we perceive and know in it
Tends to some moment's product thus,
   When a soul declares itself — to wit,
By its fruit, the thing it does! [1]

Be hate that fruit, or love that fruit,
   It forwards the general deed of man,
And each of the Many helps to recruit
   The life of the race by a general plan;
Each living his own, to boot.

I am named and known by that moment's feat;
   There took my station and degree;
So grew my own small life complete,
   As Nature obtained her best of me —
One born to love you, sweet!

And to watch you sink by the fireside now
   Back again, as you mutely sit
Musing by firelight, that great brow
   And the spirit-small hand propping it,
Yonder, my heart knows how!

So, earth has gained by one man the more,
  And the gain of earth must be heaven's gain too;
And the whole is well worth thinking o'er
  When autumn comes: which I mean to do
One day, as I said before.

"DE GUSTIBUS —" [1]

YOUR ghost [2] will walk, you lover of trees,
    (If our loves remain)
    In an English lane,
By a cornfield-side [3] a-flutter with poppies.
Hark, those two in the hazel coppice [4] —
A boy and a girl, if the good fates please,
    Making love, say, —
    The happier they!
Draw yourself up from the light of the moon,
And let them pass, as they will too soon,
    With the beanflowers' boon,
    And the blackbird's tune,
    And May, and June!

What I love best in all the world
Is a castle, precipice-encurled,
In a gash of the wind-grieved Apennine.
Or look for me, old fellow of mine,

(If I get [1] my head from out the mouth
O' the grave, and loose my spirit's bands,
And come again to the land of lands) —
In a sea-side house to the farther South,
Where the baked cicala [2] dies of drouth,
And one sharp tree — 'tis a cypress — stands
By the many hundred years red-rusted,
Rough iron-spiked, ripe fruit-o'ercrusted,
My sentinel to guard the sands
To the water's edge. For, what expands
Before the house, but the great opaque
Blue breadth of sea without a break?
While, in the house, forever crumbles
Some fragment of the frescoed walls,
From blisters where a scorpion sprawls.
A girl bare-footed brings, and tumbles
Down on the pavement, green-flesh melons,
And says there's news to-day — the king
Was shot at, touched in the liver-wing,
Goes with his Bourbon [3] arm in a sling:
— She hopes they have not caught the felons.
Italy, my Italy!
Queen Mary's saying [4] serves for me —
        (When Fortune's malice
        Lost her, Calais)

Open my heart and you will see
Graved inside of it, "Italy."
Such lovers old are I and she:
So it always was, so shall ever be!

THE ITALIAN IN ENGLAND

THAT second time they hunted me
From hill to plain, from shore to sea,
And Austria, hounding far and wide
Her blood-hounds through the country-side,
Breathed hot and instant on my trace, —
I made six days a hiding-place
Of that dry green old aqueduct
Where I and Charles,[1] when boys, have plucked
The fire-flies from the roof above,
Bright creeping through the moss they love:
— How long it seems since Charles was lost!
Six days the soldiers crossed and crossed
The country in my very sight;
And when that peril ceased at night,
The sky broke out in red dismay
With signal fires; well, there I lay
Close covered o'er in my recess,
Up to the neck in ferns and cress,

Thinking on Metternich [1] our friend,
And Charles's miserable end,
And much beside, two days; the third,
Hunger o'ercame me when I heard
The peasants from the village go
To work among the maize; you know,
With us in Lombardy, they bring
Provisions packed on mules, a string
With little bells that cheer their task,
And casks, and boughs on every cask
To keep the sun's heat from the wine;
These I let pass in jingling line,
And, close on them, dear noisy crew,
The peasants from the village, too;
For at the very rear would troop
Their wives and sisters in a group
To help, I knew. When these had passed,
I threw my glove to strike the last,
Taking the chance: she did not start,
Much less cry out, but stooped apart,
One instant rapidly glanced round,
And saw me beckon from the ground;
A wild bush grows and hides my crypt;
She picked my glove up while she stripped
A branch off, then rejoined the rest
With that; my glove lay in her breast.

Then I drew breath: they disappeared:
It was for Italy I feared.

   An hour, and she returned alone
Exactly where my glove was thrown.
Meanwhile came many thoughts; on me
Rested the hopes of Italy;
I had devised a certain tale
Which, when 'twas told her, could not fail
Persuade a peasant of its truth;
I meant to call a freak of youth
This hiding, and give hopes of pay,
And no temptation to betray.
But when I saw that woman's face,
Its calm simplicity of grace,
Our Italy's own attitude
In which she walked thus far, and stood,
Planting each naked foot so firm,
To crush the snake and spare the worm —
At first sight of her eyes, I said,
"I am that man upon whose head
They fix the price, because I hate
The Austrians over us: the State
Will give you gold — oh, gold so much! —
If you betray me to their clutch,
And be your death, for aught I know,

If once they find you saved their foe.
Now, you must bring me food and drink,
And also paper, pen and ink,
And carry safe what I shall write
To Padua, which you'll reach at night
Before the duomo [1] shuts; go in,
And wait till Tenebræ begin;
Walk to the third confessional,
Between the pillar and the wall,
And kneeling whisper, *Whence comes peace?* ·
Say it a second time, then cease;
And if the voice inside returns,
From Christ and Freedom; what concerns
The cause of Peace? — for answer, slip
My letter where you placed your lip;
Then come back happy we have done
Our mother service — I, the son,
As you the daughter of our land!"

Three mornings more, she took her stand
In the same place, with the same eyes:
I was no surer of sunrise
Than of her coming. We conferred
Of her own prospects, and I heard
She had a lover — stout and tall,
She said — then let her eyelids fall,

"He could do much" — as if some doubt
Entered her heart, — then, passing out,
"She could not speak for others, who
Had other thoughts; herself she knew:"
And so she brought me drink and food.
After four days, the scouts pursued
Another path; at last arrived
The help my Paduan friends contrived
To furnish me: she brought the news.
For the first time I could not choose
But kiss her hand, and lay my own
Upon her head — "This faith was shown
To Italy, our mother; she
Uses my hand and blesses thee."
She followed down to the sea-shore;
I left and never saw her more.

How very long since I have thought
Concerning — much less wished for — aught
Beside the good of Italy,
For which I live and mean to die!
I never was in love; and since
Charles proved false, what shall now convince
My inmost heart I have a friend?
However, if I pleased to spend
Real wishes on myself — say, three —

I know at least what one should be.
I would grasp Metternich until
I felt his red wet throat distil
In blood through these two hands. And next
— Nor much for that am I perplexed —
Charles, perjured traitor, for his part,
Should die slow of a broken heart
Under his new employers. Last
— Ah, there, what should I wish? For fast
Do I grow old and out of strength.
If I resolved to seek at length
My father's house again, how scared
They all would look, and unprepared!
My brothers live in Austria's pay
— Disowned me long ago, men say;
And all my early mates who used
To praise me so — perhaps induced
More than one early step of mine —
Are turning wise: while some opine
"Freedom grows license," some suspect
"Haste breeds delay," and recollect
They always said, such premature
Beginnings never could endure!
So, with a sullen "All's for best,"
The land seems settling to its rest.
I think then, I should wish to stand

This evening in that dear, lost land,
Over the sea the thousand miles,
And know if yet that woman smiles
With the calm smile; some little farm
She lives in there, no doubt: what harm
If I sat on the door-side bench,
And, while her spindle made a trench
Fantastically in the dust,
Inquired of all her fortunes — just
Her children's ages and their names,
And what may be the husband's aims
For each of them. I'd talk this out,
And sit there, for an hour about,
Then kiss her hand once more, and lay
Mine on her head, and go my way.

So much for idle wishing — how
It steals the time! To business now.

THE PATRIOT [1]

AN OLD STORY

IT was roses, roses, all the way,
  With myrtle mixed in my path like mad:
The house-roofs seemed to heave and sway,
  The church-spires flamed, such flags they had,
A year ago on this very day.

The air broke into a mist with bells,
   The old walls rocked with the crowd and cries.
Had I said, "Good folk, mere noise repels —
   But give me your sun from yonder skies!"
They had answered, "And afterward, what else?"

Alack, it was I who leaped at the sun
   To give it my loving friends to keep!
Naught man could do, have I left undone:
   And you see my harvest, what I reap
This very day, now a year is run.

There's nobody on the house-tops now —
   Just a palsied few at the windows set;
For the best of the sight is, all allow,
   At the Shambles' Gate — or, better yet,
By the very scaffold's foot, I trow.

I go in the rain, and, more than needs,
   A rope cuts both my wrists behind;
And I think, by the feel, my forehead bleeds,
   For they fling, whoever has a mind,
Stones at me for my year's misdeeds.

Thus I entered, and thus I go!
   In triumphs, people have dropped down dead.

"Paid by the world, what dost thou owe
   Me?" — God might question; now instead,
'Tis God shall repay: I am safer so.

THE PIED PIPER OF HAMELIN [1]

A CHILD'S STORY

I

HAMELIN [2] Town's in Brunswick,
By famous Hanover city;
   The river Weser, deep and wide,
   Washes its walls on the southern side;
   A pleasanter spot you never spied;
But, when begins my ditty,
   Almost five hundred years ago,
   To see the townsfolk suffer so
      From vermin, was a pity.

II

   Rats!
They fought the dogs and killed the cats,
   And bit the babies in the cradles,
And ate the cheeses out of the vats,
   And licked the soup from the cooks' own ladles,

Split open the kegs of salted sprats,
Made nests inside men's Sunday hats,
And even spoiled the women's chats
    By drowning their speaking
    With shrieking and squeaking
In fifty different sharps and flats.

III

At last the people in a body
    To the Town Hall came flocking:
"'Tis clear," cried they, "our Mayor's a noddy;
    And as for our Corporation — shocking
To think we buy gowns lined with ermine
For dolts that can't or won't determine
What's best to rid us of our vermin!
You hope, because you're old and obese,
To find in the furry civic robe ease?
Rouse up, sirs! Give your brains a racking
To find the remedy we're lacking,
Or, sure as fate, we'll send you packing!"
At this the Mayor and Corporation
Quaked with a mighty consternation.

IV

An hour they sat in council;
    At length the Mayor broke silence:

"For a guilder I'd my ermine gown sell,
    I wish I were a mile hence!
It's easy to bid one rack one's brain —
I'm sure my poor head aches again,
I've scratched it so, and all in vain.
Oh for a trap, a trap, a trap!"
Just as he said this, what should hap
At the chamber-door but a gentle tap?
"Bless us," cried the Mayor, "what's that?"
(With the Corporation as he sat,
Looking little though wondrous fat;
Nor brighter was his eye, nor moister
Than a too-long-opened oyster,
Save when at noon his paunch grew mutinous
For a plate of turtle green and glutinous)
"Only a scraping of shoes on the mat?
Anything like the sound of a rat
Makes my heart go pit-a-pat!"

V

"Come in!" — the Mayor cried, looking bigger:
And in did come the strangest figure!
His queer long coat from heel to head
Was half of yellow and half of red,
And he himself was tall and thin,
With sharp blue eyes, each like a pin,

And light loose hair, yet swarthy skin,
No tuft on cheek nor beard on chin,
But lips where smiles went out and in;
There was no guessing his kith and kin:
And nobody could enough admire
The tall man and his quaint attire.
Quoth one: "It's as my great-grandsire,
Starting up at the Trump of Doom's tone,
Had walked this way from his painted tombstone!"

VI

He advanced to the council-table:
And, "Please your honors," said he, "I'm able,
By means of a secret charm, to draw
All creatures living beneath the sun,
That creep or swim or fly or run,
After me so as you never saw!
And I chiefly use my charm
On creatures that do people harm,
The mole and toad and newt and viper;
And people call me the Pied [1] Piper."
(And here they noticed round his neck
A scarf of red and yellow stripe,
To match with his coat of the self-same cheque;
And at the scarf's end hung a pipe;

And his fingers, they noticed, were ever straying
As if impatient to be playing
Upon this pipe, as low it dangled
Over his vesture so old-fangled.)
"Yet," said he, "poor piper as I am,
In Tartary [1] I freed the Cham,
Last June, from his huge swarms of gnats;
I eased in Asia the Nizam
Of a monstrous brood of vampire-bats:
And as for what your brain bewilders,
If I can rid your town of rats
Will you give me a thousand guilders?"
"One? fifty thousand!" — was the exclamation
Of the astonished Mayor and Corporation.

VII

Into the street the Piper stept,
    Smiling first a little smile,
As if he knew what magic slept
    In his quiet pipe the while;
Then, like a musical adept,
To blow the pipe his lips he wrinkled,
And green and blue his sharp eyes twinkled,
Like a candle-flame where salt is sprinkled;
And ere three shrill notes the pipe uttered,
You heard as if an army muttered;

And the muttering grew to a grumbling;
And the grumbling grew to a mighty rumbling;
And out of the houses the rats came tumbling.
Great rats, small rats, lean rats, brawny rats,
Brown rats, black rats, gray rats, tawny rats,
Grave old plodders, gay young friskers,
    Fathers, mothers, uncles, cousins,
Cocking tails and pricking whiskers,
    Families by tens and dozens,
Brothers, sisters, husbands, wives —
Followed the Piper for their lives.
From street to street he piped advancing,
And step for step they followed dancing,
Until they came to the river Weser,
Wherein all plunged and perished!
— Save one who, stout as Julius Cæsar,
Swam across and lived to carry
(As he, the manuscript he cherished) [1]
To Rat-land home his commentary:
Which was, "At the first shrill notes of the pipe,
I heard a sound as of scraping tripe,
And putting apples, wondrous ripe,
Into a cider-press's gripe:
And a moving away of pickle-tub-boards,
And a leaving ajar of conserve-cupboards,
And a drawing the corks of train-oil-flasks,

And a breaking the hoops of butter-casks:
And it seemed as if a voice
(Sweeter far than by harp or by psaltery
Is breathed) called out, 'Oh rats, rejoice!
The world is grown to one vast drysaltery!
So munch on, crunch on, take your nuncheon,[1]
Breakfast, supper, dinner, luncheon!'
And just as a bulky sugar-puncheon,
All ready staved, like a great sun shone
Glorious scarce an inch before me,
Just as methought it said, 'Come, bore me!'
— I found the Weser rolling o'er me."

VIII

You should have heard the Hamelin people
Ringing the bells till they rocked the steeple.
"Go," cried the Mayor, "and get long poles,
Poke out the nests and block up the holes!
Consult with carpenters and builders,
And leave in our town not even a trace
Of the rats!" — when suddenly, up the face
Of the Piper perked in the market-place,
With a, "First, if you please, my thousand guilders!"

IX

A thousand guilders! The Mayor looked blue;
So did the Corporation too.

For council dinners made rare havoc
With Claret, Moselle, Vin-de-Grave, Hock;
And half the money would replenish
Their cellar's biggest butt with Rhenish.
To pay this sum to a wandering fellow
With a gypsy coat of red and yellow!
"Beside," quoth the Mayor with a knowing wink,
"Our business was done at the river's brink;
We saw with our eyes the vermin sink,
And what's dead can't come to life, I think.
So, friend, we're not the folks to shrink
From the duty of giving you something for drink,
And a matter of money to put in your poke;
But as for the guilders, what we spoke
Of them, as you very well know, was in joke.
Beside, our losses have made us thrifty.
A thousand guilders! Come, take fifty!"

X

The Piper's face fell, and he cried,
"No trifling! I can't wait, beside!
I've promised to visit by dinner time
Bagdat, and accept the prime
Of the Head-Cook's pottage, all he's rich in,
For having left, in the Caliph's [1] kitchen,

Of a nest of scorpions no survivor:
With him I proved no bargain-driver,
With you, don't think I'll bate a stiver! [1]
And folks who put me in a passion
May find me pipe after another fashion."

XI

"How?" cried the Mayor, "d'ye think I brook
Being worse treated than a Cook?
Insulted by a lazy ribald
With idle pipe and vesture piebald?
You threaten us, fellow? Do your worst,
Blow your pipe there till you burst!"

XII

Once more he stept into the street,
    And to his lips again
Laid his long pipe of smooth straight cane;
    And ere he blew three notes (such sweet
Soft notes as yet musician's cunning
    Never gave the enraptured air)
There was a rustling that seemed like a bustling
Of merry crowds justling at pitching and hustling;
Small feet were pattering, wooden shoes clattering,
Little hands clapping and little tongues chattering,

And, like fowls in a farm-yard when barley is scatter-
    ing,
Out came the children running.
All the little boys and girls,
With rosy cheeks and flaxen curls,
And sparkling eyes and teeth like pearls,
Tripping and skipping, ran merrily after
The wonderful music with shouting and laughter.

XIII

The Mayor was dumb, and the Council stood
As if they were changed into blocks of wood,
Unable to move a step, or cry
To the children merrily skipping by,
— Could only follow with the eye
That joyous crowd at the Piper's back.
But how the Mayor was on the rack,
And the wretched Council's bosoms beat,
As the Piper turned from the High Street
To where the Weser rolled its waters
Right in the way of their sons and daughters!
However, he turned from South to West,
And to Koppelberg Hill his steps addressed,
And after him the children pressed;
Great was the joy in every breast.
"He never can cross that mighty top!

He's forced to let the piping drop,
And we shall see our children stop!"
When, lo, as they reached the mountain-side,
A wondrous portal opened wide,
As if a cavern was suddenly hollowed;
And the Piper advanced and the children followed
And when all were in to the very last,
The door in the mountain-side shut fast.
Did I say, all? No! One was lame,
And could not dance the whole of the way;
And in after years, if you would blame
His sadness, he was used to say, —
"It's dull in our town since my playmates left!
I can't forget that I'm bereft
Of all the pleasant sights they see,
Which the Piper also promised me.
For he led us, he said, to a joyous land,
Joining the town and just at hand,
Where waters gushed and fruit-trees grew
And flowers put forth a fairer hue,
And everything was strange and new;
The sparrows were brighter than peacocks here,
And their dogs outran our fallow deer,
And honey-bees had lost their stings,
And horses were born with eagles' wings:
And just as I became assured

My lame foot would be speedily cured,
The music stopped and I stood still,
And found myself outside the hill,
Left alone against my will,
To go now limping as before,
And never hear of that country more!"

XIV

Alas, alas for Hamelin!
    There came into many a burgher's pate
    A text which says that heaven's gate
    Opes to the rich at as easy rate
As the needle's eye takes a camel in!
The Mayor sent East, West, North and South,
To offer the Piper, by word of mouth,
    Wherever it was men's lot to find him,
Silver and gold to his heart's content,
If he'd only return the way he went,
    And bring the children behind him.
But when they saw 'twas a lost endeavor,
And Piper and dancers were gone forever,
They made a decree that lawyers never
    Should think their records dated duly
If, after the day of the month and year,
These words did not as well appear,
"And so long after what happened here

On the twenty-second of July,
Thirteen hundred and seventy-six:"
And the better in memory to fix
The place of the children's last retreat,
They called it, the Pied Piper's Street —
Where any one playing on pipe or tabor
Was sure for the future to lose his labor.
Nor suffered they hostelry or tavern
    To shock with mirth a street so solemn;
But opposite the place of the cavern
    They wrote the story on a column,
And on the great church-window painted
The same, to make the world acquainted
How their children were stolen away,
And there it stands to this very day.
And I must not omit to say
That in Transylvania [1] there's a tribe
Of alien people who ascribe
The outlandish ways and dress
On which their neighbors lay such stress,
To their fathers and mothers having risen
Out of some subterraneous prison
Into which they were trepanned [2]
Long time ago in a mighty band
Out of Hamelin town in Brunswick land,
But how or why, they don't understand.

XV

So, Willy, let me and you be wipers
Of scores out with all men — especially pipers!
And, whether they pipe us free fróm rats or fróm
　　mice,
If we've promised them aught, let us keep our
　　promise!

INSTANS TYRANNUS [1]

I

OF the million or two, more or less,
I rule and possess,
One man, for some cause undefined,
Was least to my mind.

II

I struck him, he grovelled of course —
For, what was his force?
I pinned him to earth with my weight
And persistence of hate:
And he lay, would not moan, would not curse,
As his lot might be worse.

III

"Were the object less mean, would he stand
At the swing of my hand!

For obscurity helps him and blots
The hole where he squats."
So, I set my five wits on the stretch
To inveigle the wretch.
All in vain! Gold and jewels I threw,
Still he couched there perdue; [1]
I tempted his blood and his flesh,
Hid in roses my mesh,
Choicest cates [2] and the flagon's best spilth:
Still he kept to his filth.

IV

Had he kith now or kin, were access
To his heart, did I press:
Just a son or a mother to seize!
No such booty as these.
Were it simply a friend to pursue
'Mid my million or two,
Who could pay me in person or pelf [3]
What he owes me himself!
No: I could not but smile through my chafe:
For the fellow lay safe
As his mates do, the midge and the nit,
— Through minuteness, to wit.

V

Then a humor more great took its place
At the thought of his face,
The droop, the low cares of the mouth,
The trouble uncouth
'Twixt the brows, all that air one is fain
To put out of its pain.
And, "no!" I admonished myself,
"Is one mocked by an elf,
Is one baffled by toad or by rat?
The gravamen's [1] in that!
How the lion, who crouches to suit
His back to my foot,
Would admire [2] that I stand in debate!
But the small turns the great
If it vexes you, — that is the thing!
Toad or rat vex the king?
Though I waste half my realm to unearth
Toad or rat,'tis well worth!"

VI

So, I soberly laid my last plan
To extinguish the man.
Round his creep-hole, with never a break,
Ran my fires for his sake;

Over-head, did my thunder combine
With my underground mine:
Till I looked from my labor content
To enjoy the event.

VII

When sudden . . . how think ye, the end?
Did I say "without friend"?
Say rather, from marge to blue marge
The whole sky grew his targe [1]
With the sun's self for visible boss,
While an Arm ran across
Which the earth heaved beneath like a breast
Where the wretch was safe prest!
Do you see? Just my vengeance complete,[2]
The man sprang to his feet,
Stood erect, caught at God's skirts, and prayed.
— So, *I* was afraid!

NOTES

CAVALIER TUNES

15, 1. These three songs were included in the *Dramatic Lyrics* published in 1842 as the third number of *Bells and Pomegranates*. The third was originally entitled *My Wife Gertrude*. They have been set to music by Dr. Villiers Stanford.

" The speaker is a typical cavalier of the days of Charles I., the time is the height of the Civil War with the issue still in the balance, the place a banquet hall echoing the clash of glasses and shouts of cavaliers."

2. **Pym:** John Pym, John Hampden, Sir Arthur Hazelrig, William Fiennes, and Sir Harry Vane " the Younger " were English statesmen. Prince Rupert was a Bavarian soldier, a general in the army of his uncle, Charles I.

3. **Carles** (Dial. Eng.): Churls, rustics — in contempt.

4. **Parles** (Fr. *parler*, speak): Parleys.

16, 1. **Rouse** (Sw. *rusa*, rush): " An awakening to or a signal for action."

17, 1. **Noll:** Oliver Cromwell, England's patriot general and statesman, after Charles I's execution Lord Protector of England.

18, 1. **Flouts:** (ME. *fluyten*, jeer, play the flute): Scoff, mock.

2. **Fay:** An archaic form of *faith*.

" *HOW THEY BROUGHT THE GOOD NEWS FROM GHENT TO AIX* "

21, 1. **Pique:** The pommel of the saddle.

2. **Lokeren:** This town and the others mentioned in the

poem will be found upon any good map, in a general line from Ghent to Aix-la-Chapelle. The whole distance is about ninety miles.

3. Mecheln: The Flemish form of the more common French *Malines*.

23, 1. Dalhem: Probably *Dalheim*, a town about midway between Tongres and Aix.

2. Save Aix from her fate: The reader is to imagine that Aix has resolved upon self-destruction, rather than yield to the Spaniards.

HOME THOUGHTS, FROM THE SEA

28, 1. This poem is an expression of patriotic feeling awakened in the poet by passing the scenes of Nelson's great naval exploits.

INCIDENT OF THE FRENCH CAMP

28, 2. Ratisbon or **Regensburg:** A town on the Danube, 65 miles north of Munich, not far from the river Isar. The " incident " here described was an actual occurrence.

29, 1. My army-leader Lannes: One of Napoleon's most distinguished marshals. He commanded in the battles of Marengo, Austerlitz, Jena, Friedland, and others. For winning the battle of Montebello he was made Duke of Montebello.

2. Vans: From the French *van*, a wing. The wings of the imperial eagle upon the banner flap in the wind.

THE BOY AND THE ANGEL

32, 1. Tiring-room: "The room where the "holy vestments" are kept, with which the priests and pope are dight," *i.e.*, decked or attired. Shakespeare used the noun *tire* for *attire*.

ONE WORD MORE

35, 1. **Louvre:** The great museum in Paris.

2. **In circle:** This last picture is circular in form.

3. **Guido Reni** (1575–1642): An Italian painter.

4. **Beatrice:** Pronounce in four syllables.

37, 1. **Bice:** Pronounce in two syllables.

2. Read *Exodus* xvii.

39, 1. **Sinai-forehead:** Read *Exodus* xxiv, xxxii, and xxxiv.

2. **Jethro's daughter:** Read *Exodus* ii and iii.

40, 1. **Karshish,** etc.: These and the names two lines below are characters in his poems.

41, 1. **Fiesole:** A town on a hill above Florence.

2. **Samminiato:** In Florence.

42, 1. **Mythos:** Of the mortal whom Diana loved.

2. **Zoroaster:** Founder of the ancient Persian religion.

3. **Galileo** (1564–1642): An Italian astronomer.

4. **Aaron, Nadab, Abihu:** See *Exodus* vi and xxviii.

HERVÉ RIEL

44, 1. It is noticeable that of Browning's two grand ballads — *Hervé Riel* and *How They Brought the Good News from Ghent to Aix* — neither has an English inspiration. *Hervé Riel* records the heroism of a Breton sailor who guided the French squadron retreating from La Hogue, through the shallows of the river Rance, to a safe harborage. Browning follows history, except in one point which he overlooked — that Hervé Riel claimed holiday for life, instead of for one day.

The battle of La Hogue was fought May 19, 1692, in the war begun by Louis XIV of France to secure his succession to the Palatinate. Other powers formed a "Grand Alliance" against him, and at La Hogue, between the peninsula of La Manche and the Isle of Wight, the French fleet was defeated by the English and Dutch fleet, commanded

by Admiral Russell. This victory transferred naval suprem-
acy from France to England and Holland. Some of the
French ships which retreated to Cherbourg were taken; how
others escaped Browning here tells us.

This poem was first printed in the *Cornhill Magazine*,
March, 1871. The hundred pounds which Browning re-
ceived for it was given to a fund for the relief of Paris, then
suffering from the Franco-German war.

2. **St. Malo**, on the river Rance, and **La Hogue** are on
the north coast of Normandy.

3. **Damfreville:** The commander of the largest French ship.

45, 1. **Twelve and eighty:** A literal translation of the French
quatre-vingt-douze.

46, 1. **Plymouth:** One of the chief British naval stations.

2. **Tourville:** The French admiral.

3. **Croisickese:** An inhabitant of Le Croisic. Le Croisic,
the home of Hervé Riel, is a small fishing village on the south
coast of Brittany.

4. **Malouins:** People of St. Malo.

47, 1. **Grève:** The sands around Mont St. Michel. **Dis-
embogues** (Sp. *disemboca*): Empties.

2. **Solidor:** A fortified place on the French mainland.

49, 1. **The bay:** Of St. Michel.

2. **Rampired:** An archaic form of " ramparted "; fortified.

51, 1. **Wrack** (D. *wrak*, wrack): Ruin, destruction.

2. **Bore the bell:** Won the victory.

3. **The heroes . . . Louvre:** The heroes whose pictures
are in the Louvre, the great art gallery of Paris.

PHEIDIPPIDES

52, 1. This poem was published in *Dramatic Idyls* in 1879.
" The story stands out with something of the joyful pride
of a Greek statue among its Gothic associates."

In 490 B.C. the Persians, having razed Eretria, invaded
Attica, and camped on the plain of Marathon. The Athenian
army assembled and its generals sent a trained runner.

Philippides, or Pheidippides, to ask Lacedæmonian aid. He traversed the one hundred and forty miles between Athens and Sparta in forty-eight hours, and found the Spartans, who were celebrating their great national festival of the Carneia, backward from superstition or jealousy in joining their forces with the Athenians.

"And as to Pan, they say that Philippides (who was sent as a messenger to Lacedæmon when the Persians landed) reported that the Lacedæmonians were deferring their march; for it was their custom not to go out on a campaign till the moon was at its full. But he said that he had met with Pan near the Parthenian forest, and he had said that he was friendly to the Athenians, and would come out and help them at Marathon. Pan has been honored therefore for this message." — Pausanias in *Description of Greece*.

For full account of the battle of Marathon, consult Creasy's *Fifteen Decisive Battles*. There seems no historic foundation for the closing incident related by Browning.

This motto is the Greek: "Rejoice, we conquer." "Rejoice" was the usual Greek salutation, born of Marathon day.

2. **Dæmons** (Gr. *daimon*): Spirits.

3. **Zeus:** The supreme Greek god. **Her of the ægis and spear:** Pallas-Athene, the guardian goddess of Athens, the only deity whose authority was equal to that of Zeus. This *ægis* was a wonderful shield given to her by her father Zeus.

4. **Ye of the bow and the buskin:** Artemis and Phœbus-Apollo, whose symbols these were.

5. **Pan:** The Greek god of the woods, always represented as having the legs of a goat.

6. **Archons** (Gr. *archo*, rule): The chief magistrates of Athens after the cessation of kingly rule. **Tettix** (Gr.): A grasshopper. "The Athenians sometimes wore golden grasshoppers in their hair as badges of honor," because they thought those insects sprang from the ground, and they claimed for their ancestors similar origin.

53, 1. **Water and earth:** In token of submission.

2. **Razed:** Destroyed utterly.

54, 1. **Olumpos:** A lofty mountain in Thessaly, whose cloudy summit was believed to be the home of the gods.

55, 1. **Filleted:** Animals about to be sacrificed to the gods were adorned with garlands. Every sacrifice was accompanied by a **libation,** wine poured on the ground in honor of the deity. **Fulsome** (ME. *fulsum, ful,* full + *sum,* some). Here used with its early meaning of full, rich, not its later acquired meaning of over-rich, hence disgusting.

2. **Oak and olive and bay:** Zeus is frequently depicted with his head garlanded with oak leaves. The olive tree, symbol of peace and plenty, was sacred to Athene, as was the bay or laurel to Apollo.

56, 1. **Parnes:** These mountains were north of Athens, outside of Pheidippides' route.

2. **Fosse** (Lat. *fossa*): A ditch.

57, 1. **Ivy:** The ivy was consecrated to Pan.

2. **Wanton:** Hanging loose. Cf. *Paradise Lost,* IV, 366.

58, 1. **Greaved-thigh:** Cf. note 52, 5. Greaves were armor worn to protect the legs from knee to ankle.

2. **Fennel:** (Gr. *marathon*): A common herb. The field of Marathon was so named because overgrown with this plant. What was the significance of Pan's gift?

59, 1. **Miltiades:** The great Athenian general selected for supreme command at Marathon.

60, 1. **Akropolis** (Gr. *akros,* height + *polis,* city): The citadel of Athens.

61, 1. How did the fame of Miltiades and Themistocles decline?

MY LAST DUCHESS

62, 1. **Frà Pandolf:** An imaginary artist, as also **Claus of Innsbruck** in the last verse.

63, 1. **I gave commands:** It is not necessary to suppose that the " commands " were for her death. Prolonged cruelty would bave served his purpose. Browning, when asked what the "commands" were, called the query "a silly question," saying he had no thought of anything beyond the mere order as a revelation of character.

64, 1. **Notice Neptune:** As they are about to descend the stairs, the soulless old virtuoso calls the envoy's attention to a work of art in the courtyard below, of which he is especially proud.

UP AT A VILLA — DOWN IN THE CITY

64, 2. The whole poem is a picture of Italian life before the kingdom of Italy was formed — the Italy of nearly a century ago. It is famous for its pictures of Italian scenery as well as for its interpretation of character. The Italian nobleman of the poverty-stricken villa is as real a picture as Andrea del Sarto, or the Duke of *My Last Duchess.* Browning knew Italy and the Italians. It is worth noting how the meter is suited to the theme; its rapid movement, the prosaic effect secured in many passages, the whole so unlike the melody of *Abt Vogler* or *Saul.*

67, 1. **" The stunning cicala ":** Like the locust of our northern lands.

68, 1. **" The diligence ":** The stage coach of continental Europe; still used in parts of Italy and Switzerland.

2. **" Pulcinello ":** Punch and Judy shows, announced by a trumpeter.

3. **" Who is Dante,"** etc.: Who surpasses the greatest poets, theologians, orators, and is as great a preacher as St. Paul.

SAUL

70, 1. The first nine sections of *Saul* were printed in the seventh number of *Bells and Pomegranates* in 1845. The concluding stanzas were written in the winter of 1853–54, and the poem as enlarged was published in *Men and Women,* 1855.

The poem is based on *I Samuel* xvi, 14–23, where Saul is roused to consciousness and sanity by the music of David. This music is represented as " having three series of rising motives: first, tunes used to the brutes, sheep, quail, crickets, jerboa; second, the help-tunes of great epochs in human life, — reapers, burial, marriage, soldiers, priests; third, the songs of human aspirations, wild joys of living, fame crowning ambition and noble deeds, praise of unborn generations, the next world's reward and repose," but it is not until the culmination, the assurance of the God-love, which is the Christ, that the king is roused from his lethargy. " *Saul* is a magnificent interpretation of the old theme, a favorite with the mystics, that evil spirits are driven out by music. But in this interpretation it is not the mere tones, the thrumming on the harp, it is the religious movement of the intelligence, it is the truth of Divine love throbbing in every chord, which constitutes the spell." — *Corson.*

2. **Abner:** A Jewish general, Saul's cousin and friend.

3. **Spirit:** Melancholy and insanity were anciently attributed to evil spirits, which took possession of the afflicted persons.

72, 1. **Drear** (A.S. *dreorig*, sad): Dreary, cheerless. **Stark** (A.S. *Stearc*, stiff): Rigid.

74, 1. **Jerboa:** An Old-World rodent animal, remarkable for swift flying leaps.

75, 1. **Male-sapphire:** The ancient sapphire was the same as our lapis-lazuli.

76, 1. **Locust-flesh:** Sometimes used in Oriental countries for food.

2. **How good is man's life, the mere living:** This strikes the keynote of the whole stanza.

77, 1. Sympathy and rivalry may exist at the same time between brothers.

2. **Throe** (Scot. *thraw*): Pain, agony.

78, 1. In the edition of 1845 the last four lines of this section read thus:

" On one head the joy and the pride, even rage like the throe
   That opes the rock, helps its glad labor, and lets the
      gold go —
And ambition that sees a man lead it — oh, all of these —
   all
Combine to unite in one creature — Saul."

2. **Cherubim** (Heb. *k'rubh*): Angelic beings excelling in knowledge, next in rank to seraphim.

79, 1. David's music had served Saul an ill turn had it only roused him from lethargy to despair.

84, 1. **First King**: Cf. *I Samuel* 10.

86, 1. **Evanish**: A poetical form of vanish.

2. **Hebron**: A town sixteen miles southwest of Jerusalem.

3. **Kidron**: Kedron, a winter brook in a ravine east of Jerusalem.

4. **And behold . . . sunshine**: David pauses in his narration, which he resumes in the next section.

89, 1. Harp and song have served their turn, and David puts them aside for inspired speech. " The truth " bursts on him. Would he save Saul? Why, so would God. He cannot? But God can. And so by his human love and sympathy he realizes the divine, and prophesies the Christ. It is a tremendous inference, but nothing less is possible unless the creature's love is to excel the Creator's.

90, 1. **Purblind** (pure + blind): First, totally blind; then, dim of vision.

93, 1. **Sabaoth** (Gr. from Heb. *tsebaoth*): Armies, hosts; used chiefly in the phrase Lord God of Sabaoth.

94, 1. **Impuissance**: Want of power, inability.

2. Cf. *Rabbi Ben Ezra*:

" What I aspired to be
And was not, comforts me."

97, 1. **The whole earth . . . is so**: " Mr. Browning's most characteristic feeling for nature appears in his rendering of

those aspects of sky, or earth, or sea, of sunset, or noonday, or
dawn, which seem to acquire some sudden passionate sig-
nificance; which seem to be charged with some spiritual
secret eager for disclosure; in his rendering of those moments
which betray the passion at the heart of things, which thrill
and tingle with prophetic fire . . . when to David the
stars shoot out the pain of pent knowledge and in the gray
of the hills at morning there dwells a gathered intensity, —
then nature rises from her sweet ways of use and wont,
and shows herself the Priestess, the Pythoness, the Divinity
which she is. Or rather, through nature, the spirit of God
addresses itself to the spirit of man." — *Dowden.*

A GRAMMARIAN'S FUNERAL

97, 2. The *Grammarian's Funeral* was published in 1855 in
the volume *Men and Women*.

Grammarian is here used, not in its present narrow sense,
but with the broader meaning of a scholar, a student whose
life was devoted to letters. No particular person is indicated,
but the spirit is that which animated many a scholar — a
Scaliger, a Casaubon, a Pierre de Maricourt — of the early
Renaissance period, the Revival of Learning which, begin-
ing in Italy, spread over all Europe, and marked the transi-
tion from mediæval to modern history. The speaker is
one of the dead Grammarian's disciples who are bearing him
to the mountain top — a fit burial-place for him of lofty
aspirations. The parentheses give the leader's directions to
the corpse-bearers. Note the effect and appropriateness of
the meter, the long iambic followed by the short adonic.

3. **Crofts** (A.S. *croft*): Fields or little farms. **Thorpes** (A.S.
thorp): Villages or hamlets. **Common** and **vulgar** refer to
the ignorant and uneducated people of these crofts and
thorpes.

4. **Tether** (A.S. *teodor*, halter): Narrow bounds.

5. **Rock-row**: Mountain ridge.

98, 1. **Overcome:** Pass over; overshadow. Cf. *Macbeth* III. 4, 3.

99, 1. **Gowned him:** Took up the student life.

100, 1. **Queasy** (Norw. *kveis*, sickness after a debauch): Qualmish, nauseated.

2. **Fabric, dab brick:** Note effect of this and similar rhymes.

101, 1. **Calculus . . . him:** Diseases attacked him. **Calculus** (Lat.): The stone. **Tussis** (Lat.): A cough.

2. **Hydroptic** (Gr. *hydropikos*): Dropsical, thirsty. " Every lust is a kind of hydropic distemper, and the more we drink the more we shall thirst." — *Tillotson.*

3. **God's task . . . the earthen?** Cf. *Abt Vogler.* " On earth the broken arcs; in heaven, the perfect round."

102, 1. The keynote of this poem is Browning's favorite tenet, which the Talmud thus words: " It is not incumbent on thee to complete the work; but thou must not therefore desist from it."

2. To know the whole he would perfect himself in the minutest parts. *Hoti*, the Greek particle, ὅτι, that, etc. *Oun*, the Greek particle, οὖν, then, etc. Concerning " the doctrine of the enclitic *De*," Browning cited scholarly authority and said " that *De* meaning ' towards ' and as a demonstrative appendage is not to be confounded with the accentuated *De* meaning ' but,' was the ' doctrine ' which the Grammarian bequeathed to those capable of receiving it."

3. **Purlieus** (Lat. *per*, through + Fr. *allée*, go). Outlying districts.

103, 1. This man of lofty aspirations must have a burial-place symbolic of his past and future.

SONG FROM " PIPPA PASSES "

103, 2. Pippa's hymn strikes the keynote of the whole poem, asserting that " the service of all God's children is equally valuable in his sight."

AN EPISTLE

104, 1. *An Epistle* was begun at Rome in the winter of 1853–54, and finished later at Florence. It was published in *Men and Women*, 1855.

The poem is based on the account given in *John* ii, 1–46 of Christ's healing of Lazarus. Hardly less remarkable than the depictment of the effect of Lazarus' experience on his subsequent life is the psychological study of the learned leech, with his incredulous, science-trained intellect and his heart hungering for God's truth. Despite his protestations, we soon feel that it is to tell this strange tale of Lazarus — not to discourse of spiders and borage — that he writes to his master, and the truth breaks out at the last in that yearning eloquent cry for the God of Love.

2. **Snake-stone:** Placed upon a snake-bite, it was supposed to absorb or charm away the poison.

105, 1. **Were brought:** That is, in his last letter.

2. This gives us the date of the Epistle. Titus Flavius Vespasianus was sent by Nero in 66 to conduct the war against the Jews; when proclaimed emperor in 70 he left his son to carry on the war.

3. **Who studious . . . for a spy:** See the true spirit of the man of science, — his zeal in pursuit of knowledge, his contempt of hindering dangers.

4. **Bethany:** A village two miles from Jerusalem. The leech indicates the distance vividly and characteristically.

5. **Choler** (Gr. *chole*, bile): Here used in its original sense of bile.

6. **Spider:** Probably one of the saltigrade species, which springs on its prey like a cat or tiger. Spiders were used internally and externally for medicine down to a comparatively recent period. Sir Walter Raleigh, for instance, approved the healing virtues of a certain spider preparation.

106, 1. **Porphyry:** A hard stone used by the ancients as a mortar.

2. **Hadst:** Wouldst have. **Zoar:** One of the " cities of the plain," near the Dead Sea. Cf. *Genesis* xix, 22.

3. **Devotion is my price,** *et seq.*: Karshish protests that it is because he fears to trust his Syrian messenger with important matters that he tells the idle tale of Lazarus — thus deprecating Abib's scorn.

107, 1. **Exhibition:** Here has its medical sense — to administer a remedy.

108, 1. **Fume:** A fancy.

110, 1. **Our lord:** Some sage under whom Abib and Karshish had studied.

111, 1. **Greek fire:** This is an anachronism, as Greek fire was first used in warfare by the Byzantine Greeks against the Saracens at the siege of Constantinople in 673 A.D. Liquid fire, however, was used by the ancients. Gibbon says (Ch. 57): " It would seem that the principal ingredient was the naphtha or liquid bitumen, a light, tenacious inflammable oil, which springs from the earth and catches fire as soon as it comes in contact with the air."

115, 1. **Blue-flowering borage:** A plant valued for its stimulating medical properties. " The ancients deemed this plant one of the four 'cordial flowers' for cheering the spirits, the others being the rose, violet, and alkanet." **Aleppo:** A city of Syria.

116, 1. **Perhaps the journey's end . . . and farewell!** Karshish apologizes for dwelling at length on the case of this recovered epileptic Jew, and promises to write at leisure from Jerusalem on matters of more moment.

2. **The very God! . . . it is strange:** Art and science are thrust aside: the man's very soul cries out for God, — the God of this despised " madman."

MEETING AT NIGHT

116, 3. *Meeting at Night* and *Parting at Morning* were published in 1845 in the seventh number of *Bells and Pomegranates.* The speaker is a man who at night goes gladly home to peace and love, and at morning as gladly back to the world and work.

PROSPICE

117, 1. *Prospice* (*look forward*), written the fall after Mrs. Browning's death, was published in *Dramatis Personæ* in 1864. It expresses the poet's scorn of the idle and cowardly fear of death, and his faith in personal immortality. " Death," said Browning, when its shadow was over him, " is life, just as our daily, our momentarily dying body is none the less alive and ever recruiting new forces of existence. Without death, which is our crape-like churchyardy word for change, for growth, there could be no prolongation of that which we call life. . . . For myself, I deny death as an end of anything. Never say of me that I am dead."

2. **Arch fear:** Death.

118, 1. **Guerdon** (LL. *widerdonum*. A half translation of the OHG. *widarlon, widar,* back again + *lon,* reward.): Recompense.

2. **Brunt** (Ice. *brenna,* burn): " The ' brunt ' of the battle is the ' heat ' of the battle where it burns most fiercely." — *Trench.*

3. A beautiful allusion to his wife.

EPILOGUE TO " ASOLANDO "

118, 4. *The Epilogue to Asolando,* 1889, is " the last word spoken by Browning to the world. It is an epilogue not only to *Asolando* but to the whole of his life . . . reminds us of Browning's bracing, tonic effect upon all of us, and the hopefulness and support he has afforded many in hours of gloom or trouble. Standing apart from criticism, the poem is brave, energetic, stimulant." — *F. M. Wilson.*

Compare with this Tennyson's swan song, *Crossing the Bar.* Reread also Browning's *Prospice,* which it suggests.

119, 1. **Mawkish** (Ice. *madhkr,* maggot): Sickening, insipid.

2. **Worsted:** Defeated; have the worst of it.

3. **Fare** (A.S. *faran*, travel): Go on; often used impersonally

MY STAR

120, 1. **A certain star:** The metaphor of this suggestive little poem is thus interpreted by Mrs. Orr, in her " Handbook to Browning's Works ": " ' My Star ' may be taken as a tribute to the personal element in love; the bright peculiar light in which the sympathetic soul reveals itself to the object of its sympathy."

RABBI BEN EZRA

121, 1. **The best is yet to be:** The poet expresses the thought in *Saul* thus:

" By the spirit, when age shall o'ercome thee, thou still shalt
 enjoy
More indeed, than at first when inconscious, the life of
 a boy."

122, 1. **Irks care,** etc.: Care does not annoy, nor doubt fret, the well-fed bird or beast.

2. **Nearer we hold of God:** We possess the right or title to a nearer relationship with God.

123, 1. In *Saul* the poet says: " 'tis not what man Does which exalts him, but what man Would do."

2. **Dole:** Share, that which is dealt.

124, 1. **Its term:** Its terminus, proper end or limit.

127, 1. **Right?** Was I whom the world arraigned, or were they whom my soul disdained, right?

128, 1. **That metaphor:** Compare the same metaphor, *Isaiah* lxiv, 8 and xxix, 16; *Jeremiah* xviii, 2–6; *Romans* ix, 21.

ABT VOGLER

131, 1. The Abt or Abbé George Joseph Vogler (born at Würzburg, Bavaria, in 1749, died at Darmstadt, 1824) was a composer, professor, kapellmeister, and writer on music. Among his pupils were Weber and Meyerbeer. The " musical instrument of his invention " was called an orchestrion. " It was," says Sir G. Grove, " a very compact organ, in which four keyboards of five octaves each, and a pedal board of thirty-six keys, with swell complete, were packed into a cube of nine feet."

132, 1. **As when Solomon willed:** The reference is to legends of the Koran, which attribute to Solomon the possession of magical powers.

134, 1. **Protoplast:** " The original; the thing first formed as a copy to be imitated."

135, 1. **In sight? . . . made perfect too:** " Verses four and five are a bold attempt to describe the indescribable, to shadow forth that strange state of clairvoyance when the soul shakes itself free from all external impressions, which Vogel tells us was the case with Schubert, and which is. true of all great composers — ' whether in the body or out of the body, I cannot say.' " — *Mrs. Turnbull: Browning Soc. Papers*, Pt. IV.

2. **But here is the finger of God:** The other arts are " triumphant," but are only " art in obedience to laws "; the effects of music are allied to the miraculous.

" There is no sound in nature," says Schopenhauer, " fit to serve the musician as a model, or to supply him with more than an occasional suggestion for his sublime purpose. He approaches the original sources of existence more closely than all other artists, nay, even than Nature herself."

ANDREA DEL SARTO

141, 1. **Fiesole** (*fes'o-le*) : The ancient *Fæsulæ*, a town three miles N.E. of Florence, on a steep hill, commanding a magnificent view of the Arno Valley.

2. **As married people use:** *i.e.*, ought, or are wont to be.

142, 1. **In France:** Andrea del Sarto was summoned to the court of Francis I of France, where his painting was highly honored and handsomely remunerated. Urged by the letters from his wife, he obtained permission of the king to revisit Florence, on condition of a speedy return to his work; but he broke his pledges, and with a sum of money with which his royal patron had intrusted him, for the purchase of works of art, built the " melancholy little house " (page 148, last line), to please the soulless Lucrezia.

143, 1. **Low-pulsed forthright craftsman's hand:** "Andrea del Sarto's was, after all, but the ' low-pulsed forthright craftsman's hand,' and therefore his perfect art does not touch our hearts like that of Fra Bartolommeo, who occupies about the same position with regard to the great masters of the century as Andrea del Sarto. Fra Bartolommeo spoke from his heart. He was moved by the spirit, so to speak, to express his pure and holy thoughts in beautiful language, and the ideal that presented itself to his mind, and from which he, equally with Raphael, worked, approached almost as closely as Raphael's to that abstract beauty after which they both longed. Andrea del Sarto had no such longing; he was content with the loveliness of earth. This he could understand and imitate in its fullest perfection, and therefore he troubled himself but little about the ' wondrous paterne ' laid up in heaven. Many of his Madonnas have greater beauty, strictly speaking, than those of Bartolommeo, or even of Raphael; but we miss in them that mysterious spiritual loveliness that gives the latter their chief charm." — *Heaton's History of Painting.*

144, 1. **Morello:** The highest spur of the Apennines to the north of Florence. •

2. **What does the mountain care?** It is beyond their criticism.

3. **A man's reach should exceed his grasp:** " The true glory of art is, that in its creation there arise desires and aspirations never to be satisfied on earth, but generating new desires and new aspirations, by which the spirit of man mounts to God himself. The artist (Mr. Browning loves to insist on

this point) who can realize in marble, or in color, or in music, his ideal, has thereby missed the highest gain of art. In *Pippa Passes* the regeneration of the young sculptor's work turns on his finding that in the very perfection which he had attained lies ultimate failure. And one entire poem, *Andrea del Sarto*, has been devoted to the exposition of this thought. Andrea is 'the faultless painter'; no line of his drawing ever goes astray; his hand expresses adequately and accurately all that his mind conceives; but for this very reason, precisely because he is 'the faultless painter,' his work lacks the highest qualities of art." — *Professor Dowden.*

4. **The Urbinate . . . out of me!** Raphael Santi, born in Urbino, 1483. Though Andrea knows that Raphael is inferior to himself in technique, yet he acknowledges him to be his superior, because he reaches "above and through his art" toward heaven and things divine.

5. **George Vasari:** Friend and pupil of Michael Angelo and Andrea del Sarto, and author of *Lives of the Painters, Sculptors, and Architects.*

145, 1. **By the future:** *i.e.*, in comparison with the future.

2. **Agnolo:** Michael Angelo (or Michel Agnolo) Buonarotti.

146, 1. **For fear,** etc. : See note 1, page 142.

147, 1. **The triumph was,** etc.: The real triumph was, to have ended in your heart; that reached, the lesser triumph in France is no loss.

2. **Rafael did this,** etc.: The supposed remark of some critic.

.**151**, 1. **Leonard:** Leonardo da Vinci.

BY THE FIRESIDE

151, 2. **Is:** The present with future meaning: "Where will be thy pleasant hue?"

154, 1. **Hemp-stalks steep:** Hemp that is soaking in preparation for dressing.

2. **Fret:** The lichens ornament as with raised work.

155, 1. **Aware:** Self-conscious.

2. **My Leonor:** The "perfect wife," with the "great brow" and the "spirit-small hand," can be no other than Elizabeth Barrett Browning. The poem, though in its circumstances purely dramatic and imaginary, is autobiographic in soul. Other beautiful allusions to Mrs. Browning may be found in *One Word More, Prospice,* and *My Star.*

158, 1. **What did I say?** The description is here resumed, which was broken off at line 20, page 155.

159, 1. **Chrysolite:** Greek χρυσός and λίδος, gold-stone. Technically, a mineral substance of a pale green color.

162, 1. "With Mr. Browning," says Professor Dowden, "those moments are most glorious in which the obscure tendency of many years has been revealed by the lightning of sudden passion, or in which a resolution that changes the current life has been taken in reliance upon that insight which vivid emotion bestows; and those periods of our history are charged most fully with moral purpose, which take their direction from moments such as these." Here it is the remembrance of one of those supreme moments which determined the issue of his life, that leads the speaker of the poem to exclaim: "How the world is made for each of us!" etc.

"DE GUSTIBUS—"

163, 1. **De gustibus non est disputandum:** A Latin saying which means, "There is no disputing about tastes." This poem was published in *Men and Women* in 1855. It is a descriptive poem with a lyric and dramatic coloring. The poet, apostrophizing his friend, a lover of trees, describes the rural English scenery in contrast with the Italian landscape which he himself "loves best in all the world." His choice would be a castle among the Italian mountains, or a house by the blue sea "amidst a drought and stillness in which the very cicala dies and the cypress seems to rust."

2. **Your ghost,** etc.: The poet tells his friend that if affec-

tions persist after death his ghost will wander in an English lane in beanflower time.

3. **Cornfield-side:** Not a cornfield, but a field of wheat or similar grain.

4. **Coppice:** Thicket.

164, 1. **If I get,** etc.: If my ghost ever wanders.

2. **Cicala:** The cicada, often called the locust.

3. **Bourbon:** Descendants of the French family of Bourbon occupied at one time or another the thrones of France, Spain, and Naples. It was said of them that they "never learned or forgot anything." "Bourbonism" has become a synonym for conservatism and inaction.

4. **Queen Mary's saying:** With the loss of the town of Calais in 1558 England yielded the last of her lands on the Continent. Queen Mary is said to have declared that at her death they would find the word "Calais" written on her heart.

THE ITALIAN IN ENGLAND

This poem was written after Browning visited Italy in 1844, and it was published in *Dramatic Romances and Lyrics* in 1845 under the title *Italy in England*. The incident of the poem is not historical, but it represents with historical fidelity the struggle of the Italian liberals against Austrian oppression. An Italian rebel, who is an exile in England, tells the story. It is reported that Mr. Browning remembered with pride the fact that Mazzini read this poem to his fellow exiles in England in order to show how an Englishman could sympathize with them.

165, 1. **Charles:** Charles Albert, Prince of Carignano, first supported the Italian revolutionary movement, but later abandoned it. It is quite possible that as a boy he played with the exile, for he was brought up in a simple democratic way.

166, 1. **Metternich:** A man of iron nerve and will who, as foreign minister of Austria, was prominent in guarding

Austria's interests in Italy and in repressing all attempts toward Italian liberty.

168, 1. Duomo: Cathedral. **Tenebræ** (next line): A religious service usually sung in the afternoon or evening; it was customary to darken the church. (Lat. *tenebræ*, darkness.)

THE PATRIOT

171, 1. This poem tells "an old story," though a purely fictitious one as Browning states. A year ago the patriot entered the city honored, and now, after having served his people with his customary devotion, he must die disgraced. Those whom he served have proved fickle; but the reward which men refused he will receive from the hand of God.

THE PIED PIPER OF HAMELIN

173, 1. *The Pied Piper* was written for the small son of the actor, William Macready, to amuse the boy during an illness by furnishing an interesting story for him to illustrate. Browning seems to have thought the poem of little value; it is said that he did not intend it for publication and it was only at the editor's request that the poem was supplied to fill out the volume of *Dramatic Lyrics*, published in 1842. The story is classed as a myth, and the piper is allied to Goethe's Erlking and also to Hermes and Orpheus. The piper's pipe recalls the pipe of Orpheus, the lyre of Apollo, and even the harp of Jack of the Beanstalk, which he stole from the ogre.

2. **Hamelin:** A town in Prussia near Hanover.

176, 1. **Pied:** Having spots and patches of various color. So also *piebald* in stanza XI.

177, 1. **Tartary:** An indefinite region in Europe or Asia. **Cham:** A title applied to various oriental rulers. **Nizam:** A title of the native ruler of Haidarabad in India.

178, 1. **The manuscript he cherished:** These lines refer to a legend that Cæsar, when compelled to leave his sinking ship at the siege of Alexandria, swam with one arm while he held his manuscript of the *Commentaries on the Gallic Wars* above the water with the other. Froude says this statement is "more absurd than legends usually are."

179, 1. **Nuncheon:** An obsolete or dialectic word meaning light nourishment taken between meals.

180, 1. **Caliph:** A title given to the successors of Mohammed, claimed especially by the Sultan of Turkey.

181, 1. **Stiver:** A Dutch coin worth about two cents.

185, 1. **Transylvania:** A province in southeastern Hungary.

2. **Trepanned:** An obsolete or archaic word meaning trapped; generally spelled *trapan'*.

INSTANS TYRANNUS

186, 1. The title means "The Threatening Tyrant." The poem is "the confession of a king, who has been possessed by an unreasoning and uncontrolled hatred for one man. This man was his subject, but so friendless and obscure that no hatred could touch, so stupid or so upright that no temptation could lure him into his enemy's power. The king became exasperated by the very smallness of the creature which thus kept him at bay; drew the line of persecution closer and closer; and at last ran his victim to earth. But, at the critical moment, the man so long passive and cowering threw himself on the protection of God. The king saw, in a sudden revulsion of feeling, an Arm thrown out from the sky, and the 'wretch' he had striven to crush, safely enfolded in it. Then he in his turn—was 'afraid.'"—*Mrs. Sutherland Orr.*

"A faint vein of humor runs through the poem. The king describes what has been; his hatred has passed. He sees how small and fanciful it was, and the illustrations he uses to express it tell us that; though they carry with them also the contemptuous intensity of his past hatred. The swell of the hatred remains . . . God has intervened, and the worst of it has passed away."—*Stopford A. Brooke.*

The poem shows how the evil passions, though too long having their own way, are at last checked by the higher moral power—the power of conscience in human nature.

187, 1. **Perdue** (Fr. *perdue,* pp. of *perdre,* to lose): Lost to view, hidden.

2. **Cates:** Dainty food. Cf. *cater;* to buy or provide (food). **Spilth** is an archaic word meaning something spilled or freely poured out.

3. **Pelf:** Money, riches; originally meaning stolen property.

188, 1. **Gravamen** (Lat. *gravis,* heavy; *gravare,* to load, burden): Grievance.

2. **Admire:** Wonder.

189, 1. **Targe:** Shield or defence. **Boss** (next line) means a knob on the shield.

2. **Just my vengence complete:** Just as my vengence was complete.

QUESTIONS AND TOPICS FOR STUDY

1. Insistence on sense before sound.
2. Condensation and concentration of thought.
3. Singular power of adapting meter to thought. Note:
    a. Cavalier Tunes.
    b. A Grammarian's Funeral.
    c. Saul.
4. Use of feminine endings.
    a. Memorabilia.
    b. By the Fireside.
5. Blank verse.
    a. Among the best in the English language.
    b. Full of dramatic vigor.
6. So-called obscurities.
    a. Due to depth of thought.
    b. Due to condensation, to the effort to say much in few words.
    c. Usually easily explained by study of constructions.

Study of the Poems

CAVALIER TUNES

In all study of Browning we should be peculiarly alive to the dramatic quality of the poet's work. He was a student of the great drama of humanity. Abstract beauty made little appeal to him; life — full, vigorous, among a world of men and women — was to him the true subject for the poet's pen. In the person

214

of his characters, he lived through the varied experiences of humanity. For that reason his so-called lyric poems have strongly-marked dramatic quality, and many, if not all, may be called dramatic monologues. Even in the "Cavalier Tunes," which are essentially songs, the dramatic element is strongly marked. The student should characterize the speaker in each of the songs.

I

1. What is the function of a refrain in a song?   How is the refrain, or chorus, in this song made a part of it?
2. What is the meter of the poem?   Discuss its fitness for the poem.

II

1. What metrical peculiarity is there in this song?
2. How does the speaker reveal his fortunes; his indebtedness to the King; his character?

III

1. What Cavalier traits does the third song show?   How has Browning revealed the man to us without a word of actual description?
2. Characterize these as patriotic songs, dwelling on *a.* Singing quality; *b.* Vigor; *c.* Spirit; *d.* Power to inspire.

THE LOST LEADER

1. Consult a story of Wordsworth's life and give an account of the circumstances leading to the act here censured.
2. What is meant by the "handful of silver," and the "riband to stick in his coat"?   What was the "one gift of which Fortune bereft us"?   What did Wordsworth gain, what lose, by his action?
3. What shall be the worst punishment for the Lost Leader?
4. If the poem had been written of you or some one dear to you,

what would have hurt most in it? Justify the statement that it is "a poem which does the work of swords."

GOOD NEWS FROM GHENT

1. What is the meter? Its value in the poem?
2. Discuss the value of the abrupt beginning. When is the full import of their ride first revealed?
3. Who is the real hero of the poem?
4. Select examples of run-on lines and show the advantage gained by their use.
5. Select striking examples of simile, metaphor, alliteration.

EVELYN HOPE

1. Give a general characterization of the speaker and of Evelyn Hope.
2. What is the poet's conception of death and a future life as shown in Stanzas II and VII?

HOME THOUGHTS

1. Discuss irregularities of meter in the first poem, telling whether you think them good or not.
2. Discuss the closing lines of this poem, commenting especially on their abruptness. Is it a fault? Why?
3. Comment on the rhythm of the second poem; on the rhyme used. Why is it not varied?

INCIDENT OF THE FRENCH CAMP

1. What do you understand by the term "dramatic monologue"? Who is the speaker in this poem?
2. Characterize Napoelon as seen here.
3. In the picture of the boy, what characteristics of the French soldiers who conquered Europe are made evident?
4. Comment on this poem as a narrative.

THE BOY AND THE ANGEL

1. Retell the story in as few words as possible, yet completely.
2. What was lacking in the praise offered by Gabriel in Theocrite's place?
3. Would it have been better to tell the events given in Stanzas XXV–XXX, in place of the brief Stanza X? Why?
4. What is shown of human responsibility, even in the least act, in Stanza XXXIII–XXXVII?

ONE WORD MORE

Nettleship, in his *Essays on Browning's Poetry*, gives the following preface: "Every artist who 'lives and loves' a woman truly, desires to honor her by employing some highest attribute of his nature, one unknown to the world, which shall produce for her a work to be all her own, — for her heart only. The world sees, knows, often misjudges, his other work. She who loves him takes this tribute of his inner soul, and by her sympathy urges him on to better work for the world."

1. What does the poem tell us of the wife who could so inspire Browning?
2. Who was Dante? Tell the story of Beatrice.
3. State in your own words Stanza VIII.
4. Explain Stanza X. Is it true?
5. Tell in your own words the meaning of Stanza XIII.
6. What does Stanza XIV show of Browning's belief as to the poet's relation to his characters?

HERVÉ RIEL

1. Select passages where much is told in a few words; passages containing vivid figures.
2. Compare with "Good News from Ghent" and "Incident of the French Camp" for vividness, dramatic power, and clear presentation of character.
3. What is the meter? Discuss its fitness for such a poem.

Compare with the two poems mentioned. Would "Hervé Riel" gain or lose by using the meter of either of the others? Why? Study especially Stanza V.

4. Characterize the chief actor, Hervé Riel. What would have been lost had Browning followed history and made him ask holiday for life?

PHEIDIPPIDES

1. Show how the meter is especially suited to the theme.
2. Why does he name and claim Pan as "patron — coequal in praise" with Zeus or Apollo?
3. Why would the wide world stand "spitting at Sparta" if Athens should fall?
4. Why does he reproach his gods as he turns homeward? Why does he turn aside to worship the gods in the "wild waste tract" of Parnes?
5. How did Pan keep his promise to Pheidippides?

MY LAST DUCHESS

Alexander considers this "one of the most perfect of dramatic monologues. Two characters are revealed — a beautiful, innocent girl, fresh from her convent school, full of the joy of life, married to a cold, selfish egoist, hateful himself and hating happiness in others. He sets to work to repress her joy in life, to force her into his own mold,— and breaks her heart. He reveals her, and unconsciously, himself to the messenger who has come to enter into negotiations concerning the Duke's second marriage."

What does the Duke's comment on the portrait show of his estimate of the Duchess? What does it reveal of himself?

UP AT A VILLA — DOWN IN THE CITY

1. What is the character of the speaker? Cite passages on which you base your opinion.
2. What is his conception of the joy of living?

CPSIA information can be obtained at www.ICGtesting.com
Printed in the USA
BVOW032003050812

297041BV00001B/164/A

9 781434 492562